SECRET NASHVILLE

A GUIDE TO THE WEIRD, WONDERFUL, AND OBSCURE

Mason Douglas

Reedy Press
PO Box 5131
St. Louis, MO 63139
www.reedypress.com

Library of Congress Control Number: 2018945689
ISBN: 9781681061757

Design by Jill Halpin
Unless otherwise indicated, all photos are courtesy of the author
or in the public domain.

Printed in the United States of America
18 19 20 21 22 5 4 3 2 1

DEDICATION

For Kim . . . and the way we always love seeing
what's on the next page.

CONTENTS

INTRODUCTION

As they say, the times they are a-changing! And Nashville, Tennessee, arguably the biggest "It" city in America in recent years, is no stranger to these changing times. Music City is a bustling metropolis of downtown neon honkytonks, overflowing tour busses, bachelorette parties, easygoing pedal taverns, and the new home to every genre of music imaginable, let alone its famous flagship Country genre. It's a given that tourists will get their selfies in front of the full-scale Parthenon, take in the facade of the Ryman, hit the Grand Ole Opry, and maybe take a tour of the Country Music Hall of Fame—these go-to classics are a necessity for any visitor, and the locals would question anyone who didn't see these famous landmarks.

But these well-known attractions only scratch the surface.

There is a deep Nashville underground: the hidden legacies that only the natives know with fuzzy memories. The mysteries that time and coats of paint are trying to mask over. The secrets.

Secret Nashville helps bring to light a few of these mysteries and buried clues to Nashville's past, along with the treasures that are hidden in plain sight. And much like a typical tour of the city, these items are only the tip of the iceberg: there have been millions of songs, stories, and experiences that have shaped the town that won't be heard on any tour of the city and this first edition is a mere fraction. But history isn't slowing down for anyone, so let's jump in! This is your party bus to the unknown and the forgotten enigmas of history of Music City.

Now let's go tell some secrets . . .

—Mason

1 ACKLEN POST OFFICE WALL OF FAME

How did this wall at the Acklen Post Office get started?

Tucked away around a few turns in the Hillsboro area is the Acklen Post Office, a nondescript postal service center that looks pretty much like all the others around town. One step inside this one, though, and it becomes obvious that it's a little different. For decades now, various country music artists of all levels—from legends like Garth Brooks, Crystal Gayle, and Alan Jackson to the lesser knowns—have provided personalized headshots to the post office, where they've been framed and densely arranged to cover the entire western wall of the interior.

Nestled right in Music Row, the Acklen P.O. is frequented daily by musicians, producers, artists, and label execs, so it's no surprise that they would want to be promoting their talent to every passerby possible. Although no employee knows how it all began, the genesis of the collection seems to go back to the early '80s, based on a few clues within the pictures, like the labels certain artists (such as Nanci Griffith and the Nitty Gritty Dirt Band) were on at the time of their submitted headshots. Most likely, the employees simply began asking the superstars for their autographs and then hung them in the office for the customers to gawk at, where the gawking continues today. The collection has grown over time and still has a new shot pop up now and then, squeezing in around the competition or just flat-out replacing a long-forgotten up-and-comer.

Many a celebrity has been spotted sending and picking up packages in this particular post office.

Top: The Acklen Post Office Wall
Inset: Jeff Carson and Billy Dean keeping watch

WALL OF FAME

WHAT Acklen Post Office

WHERE 2006 Acklen Ave.

COST Free to enter

PRO TIP For any songwriter or artist new to town, get a P.O. Box at this location—the 37212 area code is the one for Music Row and will go a long way toward making you legit.

2 ANDREW JACKSON'S HAIR

Wait . . . is that really A. J.'s hair?

The Tennessee State Museum may boast a wide number of artifacts, from mastodon bones discovered in local rivers to Indian sculptures and pottery, all the way to a 3,600-year-old mummy . . . but there is one display that often gets missed by museum-goers and stops the ones who see it right in their tracks. In a small display case engulfed by a much bigger display case of more visible items is a small tuft of Andrew Jackson's real life, no kidding, hair. This lock of white is from the head of one of the most famous (or infamous, depending on who you talk to) presidents in history and is right there, within inches of any onlooker.

A. J.'S HISTORIC HAIR

WHAT Tennessee State Museum

WHERE 1000 Rosa L Parks Blvd.

COST Free

PRO TIP Allow at least 2 hours to walk through the museum

There is no known story on how it came into the museum's or the collector's possession—apparently, it was not uncommon at the time to possess a few strands of Jackson's coif in a locket, so it could simply be one of many that were hidden in attic chests and nightstand drawers. There are other Jackson-related items of interest, like his top hat, but the real draw is the passing glimpse and the unassuming exhibit of his ivory mane.

. . . And maybe the mummy.

The old Tennessee State Museum

Be on the lookout for Sam Davis's "Shoe of Doom," where the Boy Hero of the Confederacy hid the stolen documents that led to his execution and martyrdom.

3 ARTSY BIKE RACKS

Wait . . . that's a bike rack?!

With further exploration of Nashville, one might notice that there are a few abstract sculptures on random street corners . . . so what gives? Even to locals, it seems like these are just haphazard metal concoctions, brainchildren of local artists designed to catch the eye on the ride by. However, the reality is that a number of these structures serve a more functional aesthetic purpose—these are actually very artistic bike racks. Commissioned over three phases between 2010 and 2012 as a Metro Arts initiative toward healthy living, there are some 21 very clever options to chain up to, such as the *Soundboard Sliders* at 2318 12th Ave South, *Capital* and *Corn and Tomato* at the Farmers' Market, and *Are We There Yet?* at 2500 Charlotte Avenue.

BIKE RACK ART

WHAT Unexpected art on the corner

WHERE All over town, but *Microphone* is at the northeast corner of Demonbreun and Music Row

COST Free

PRO TIP You probably already know this, but it's best to lock your wheel AND the frame of your bike for the most effective protection.

The most popular chain bait is *Microphone,* right by Music Row at the top of Demonbreun Hill. At any given moment this giant microphone, designed by Franne Lee, Keith Harmon, and Mac Hill, is there for wannabe rock stars and huge voices needing the right backdrop for their larger-than-life selfie. Oddly enough, there aren't a whole lot of bikes on it the majority of the time.

Top left: Microphone
Top right: Soundboard Sliders
Above left: Are We There Yet?

Don't miss *Good Eats*, a giant and very random kitchen whisk on the corner of Broadway and 21st Avenue.

<u>4</u> BANK STREET

Is that road a brick wall?

There's a short stretch of road downtown that contains an anomaly not quite matching the rest of the semi-smooth asphalt roads winding through the city center. Connecting 1st and 2nd Avenues just north of Church is a road that used to be known as Clark Alley and has what pretty much looks like a horizontal brick wall as its design.

These small bricks are called "setts" (or Belgian block), which are similar to cobblestones but more rectangular (cobblestones are typically rounded and more irregular in shape), fit closer together (allowing a smoother, quieter ride), and provide more traction to traversing horses. This is the last remaining street in Nashville that still has these over-160-year-old setts intact— the short length and infrequent use put it low on the priority list for repaving. But that neglect helped it be designated a Historical Landmark in August 2015. Today, most of the traffic isn't drag-racing and shredding the blocks beneath the tires—it's mainly slow-strolling rubberneckers praying that one of the metered spots is open and trying to find a dang place to park. It's a prime spot for downtown employees and those in the know trying to avoid the twenty dollar garages.

GAME, "SETT," AND MATCH

WHAT The last cobblestone street downtown

WHERE 189 Bank Street

COST Free

PRO TIP 1st Ave, right on the corner, contains a statue of the city's founding, as well as a replica of Fort Nashborough, the original stockade settlement of the city.

The last setts of Bank Street

In the one-hundred-year flood in 2010, Bank Street was a number of feet under water as the water crept up past 3rd Avenue.

5 BATMAN BUILDING EARS

What's up with the ears of that building downtown?

Make no mistake about it, whenever a visitor sees the skyline of Nashville, the first thing they notice is the unique shape of the AT&T Building, known very casually as "The Batman Building." With a normal thirty-three-floor skyscraper body, the defining characteristics are the ears — yep, the building has ears! It's so recognizable that you almost expect to the see the Bat Signal lighting up the sky behind it.

So how did it get this unique architecture? The history goes back to a 1990 blueprint by Earl Swensson Associates Inc., one of 39 alternative versions that were considered for the right signature design. In looking down at the models, senior architect Dick Miller says he never even saw the Batman resemblance: "When you look at a small model, you never realize that aspect. I like it. I remember the client bringing the Batmobile there one time to stage an event."

And Earl Swensson himself describes the ears: "We found out that there was an outfit down in Texas, (because we had some consultants from there), that had towers down there that could lease them to various stations. So we had WSM and WLAC and we went 'Boy, that could make some real money,' so we designed it to do that. And we had it all set up, and they were going to lease those towers, and then the lawyers said, 'No you can't do that.' We said, 'Why?' They said because we can't allow people into the building. So, we couldn't do it but that's why that's there."

The ears of the building were digitally removed from the skyline when downtown Nashville was used in the opening scene of *The Matrix*.

THE BATMAN BUILDING

WHAT Nashville's most recognizable skyline feature

WHERE 333 Commerce St.

COST Free to look at from outside

PRO TIP Never call it "The AT&T Building." Just don't do it.

The antenna ears of Batman Building

The Batman ears should be giant radio towers, appropriately transmitting the hits and misses of the surrounding music industry but instead sharpen the jagged edges of the Nashville skyline.

6 BEAR CAVE

Why is there a bear cave in a front yard, and where is it?

This is a pretty well-kept secret and hasn't quite made it into the everyday rumor mill of Nashville pop culture. But yes, it does exist, and we'll take you there right now! Down in Green Hills, on an unassuming line of streets developed into a typical neighborhood of houses full of families, are the remnants of an amusement park from long ago, the Glendale Park Zoo.

Owned by Percy Warner himself and built in 1912 as a way to entice people to use his Glendale streetcar, it had a full-on carousel, the thrill rides of the time, shooting galleries, roller skating, croquet and tennis, and of course, a zoo, which featured an alligator pit, some buffalo, ostriches, monkeys, peacocks, and a bear den with two residents, Zana and Zerle.

The park closed in 1932, as a result of the Depression and the blossoming automobile business, which shouldered out the streetcar industry. The ruins aren't easy to see but if you look closely, you can find telltale signs that tell the story.

In the front yard of a house set back from Scenic Drive is a depression in the ground and the upper section of the stone cave that used to house the bears. Also on the same property are stairs and paths that were the entrance to the park itself, which have been modified to fit into the outside walkways. Up the street, where Scenic turns into Tower Place, a random wall rises out of the ground on the north side of the turn, which

IT'S A ZOO OUT THERE!

WHAT Neighborhood bear cave

WHERE 4310 Scenic Drive

COST Free

PRO TIP In order to avoid creepiness and possibly jailtime, do not step onto the grass of the house—that's called trespassing. Pictures and viewing are from the street only.

Top: The Glendale Park Zoo bear cave
Inset: Ruins of the old streetcar station

was part of the streetcar infrastructure. And across the street from that, near 1008 Tower Place, is a creepy random concrete staircase leading to nowhere, which was the same staircase the patrons would descend to enter the park after stepping off the streetcar.

The Glendale Park Zoo was Nashville's first official zoo.

7 BICENTENNIAL PARK DESIGN—PART 1

Is there any rhyme or reason to the design of this park?

When the Bicentennial Capitol State Park just north of the downtown Capitol was opened in 1996, it wasn't just a patch of grass and some picnic tables—there was a tremendous amount of forethought and historical tribute that went into the layout of this Nashville gem. The availability of the nineteen acres that it sits on were a stroke of luck; progress had built up houses and skyscrapers around the Capitol over time, but the north side was always deemed too swampy for efficient building. But it was perfect for the park needed to pay tribute to the two-hundred-year celebration of statehood.

There is far more than meets the eye on a stroll around the park, so let's reveal its secrets. Starting on the north end of the park, one first notices the giant two-hundred-foot granite map of Tennessee embedded in the concrete, thought to be the largest map of the state in existence. Just past that, are the Rivers of Tennessee Fountains, which include thirty-one vertical fountains representing each of Tennessee's thirty-one main waterways and is always a cool refresher for children during the summer. Even the flags in this plaza are steeped with meaning: sixteen smaller state flags represent Tennessee being the 16th state inducted into the Union, and the two larger state flags represent one hundred years of statehood each.

NOT YOUR EVERYDAY PARK

WHAT Bicentennial Park

WHERE 600 James Robertson Parkway

COST Free

PRO TIP Street parking is available, but insiders park at the Farmers' Market and make that part of their park visit.

14

Left: Bicentennial Park
Right: Tennessee flags within the park

Passing under the tracks on the left (west) side of fountains and into the park, you'll walk past a two-thousand-seat amphitheater modeled after the Greek theater in Epidaurus and boasting unparalleled views of the Capitol and downtown skyline looming over the event performers. Just past the open-air venue will be the Statehood Memorial, which has the McNairy Spring bubbling out of the ground and marking the spot of one of the original springs that attracted pioneer Timothy Demonbreun.

Although not technically part of the park, the Nashville Farmers' Market sits adjacent to the park and provides some unique culinary options as well as farm-fresh veggies and local gifts—well worth the stop.

BICENTENNIAL PARK DESIGN—PART 2

What about the wall?

Now for the most tremendous accomplishment of the park design: the Pathway of History. This 1,400-foot wall is engraved with centuries of history, starting in prehistoric times and getting more detailed within the past two hundred years, each ten-year period marked by a granite pylon and anniversary monuments at the 1796 and 1896 points. Eagle eyes will notice the broken up sections in the wall representing the Civil War, a period of extreme division in the state.

The World War II Memorial is next along the stroll, with monolithic tributes, concrete inlays, and a giant 18,000-pound granite globe floating on one-eighth inch of water.

At the southern end of the park is the perfect shot: the capitol building at the pinnacle, with the entire stretch of grounds unfolding beneath it, the iconic Court of 3 Stars in the foreground. This will be the photo that ends up framed on your wall, getting the most likes on your socials, and sliding by on a screensaver. The Court of 3 Stars has the three stars of the Tennessee flag (one for each region) painted on the concrete base and is also surrounded by the striking 95-Bell Carillon. Each bell represents one of the 95 counties

A bike path jutting off from the east side of the park will take the rider to and past the site of the Sulphur Spring, whose waters follow a meandering path back to the Cumberland.

The 95-Bell Carillon

in Tennessee and together they provide a musical tribute to the area: Every hour, the bells chime a Tennessee-themed song, to which a 96th bell, located in the capitol building, answers with a final chime.

Back down the eastern walk of the park is the Walkway of Counties, showing the topography of each section of the state, with native foliage from each section represented. Note the circles in the concrete: these are time capsules from each county in the state, which will be opened in 2096 at the tricentennial celebration.

MORE SECRETS . . .

WHAT Bicentennial Park

WHERE 600 James Robertson Parkway

COST Free

PRO TIP The giant globe in the World War II Memorial is actually spinnable with some elbow grease put into it.

9 BIRTHPLACE OF THE OPRY

Where did the Opry start?

All right, pay attention to this one—this is important. And it's also something you're not going to see or hear on any tour around Nashville. It's well known that the Ryman hosted the Grand Ole Opry for thirty years until the Grand Ole Opry House opened in '74. But the Grand Ole Opry has been in operation since 1925. So where did it play for twenty years before it went to the Ryman? And more important, where did it start?

A brief history: the ongoing radio show has been held at the Belcourt Theater (then the Hillsboro Theater), the Dixie Tabernacle in East Nashville, and the War Memorial Auditorium. But the first ever location of the Opry was at the National Life and Accident Insurance Company building on the northwest corner of 7th and Union in downtown Nashville.

It was in this building that WSM was started, that George Hay put together the "Barn Dance" program, and where the name was changed to the "Grand Ole Opry" in 1927. It's the pure history from this single location that changed Nashville and defined country music, if not arguably ALL music, for future generations.

The iconic structure is gone now; it's the parking lot of the Tennessee Tower government building and can only tell its secrets from the written records gathering dust in the archives.

It was also in this building that Fred Rose met a man named Hank Williams, who had a few songs he wanted to play for him and, well . . . the rest is history.

Top: The site of the birth of the Grand Ole Opry
Inset: Historical marker for Edwin W. Craig

PAVED PARADISE AND PUT UP A PARKING LOT

WHAT The original location of the Opry

WHERE Northwest corner of 7th Ave. and Union St.

COST Free

PRO TIP The courtyard is great place to get a view of the interior parking lot and is open to the public.

10 BISON MEADOW

Why are those bushes walking around?

It's pretty much guaranteed that hundreds of locals pass a certain corner in Forest Hills and never even observe the strange anomaly that looks like it's observing them from the corner. At first glance, it just looks like a bunch of random bushes scattered throughout an overgrown field, but a closer look will show that these bushes are topiary shaped like bison, with size-appropriate legs, heads, and musculature. Once you see them, they become impossible not to notice, and you'll be slightly annoyed that every bush in the world now looks like a bison to you.

The park itself is Bison Meadow, full of flora from the days when the bison out populated any humans in the area, with passionflower, ironweed, rudbeckia, and other native wildflowers covering the two acre area. It lies on an old portion of the Natchez Trace, the trail the Native Indians of the area, as well as the settlers, used to travel up from Mississippi. Animals like the bison also used it to make their way to the salt lick by the Cumberland. The bushes are technically Hicks Yew shrubs once planted beneath and now engulfing the bison-shaped metal wire frames designed by Alan LeQuire of *Athena* and *Musica* fame.

Today, the park is a quiet escape from the hustle and bustle, perfect for a picnic or a quick meditation amongst the ever-silent buffalo.

Just around the corner is Taylor Swift's Nashville home at 2201 Harding Place.

Top: One of the many topiary bison exploring the meadow

OVER THE RIVER AND THROUGH THE WOODS . . .

WHAT Bison Meadow Park

WHERE Northwest corner of Hillsboro and Tyne

COST Free

PRO TIP Park in the tiny lot off Hemingway Drive, just north of the park

<u>11</u> BOBBY'S IDLE HOUR

New Nashville is cool . . . but can we get a taste of the good ol' days?

Jeans have replaced Wranglers, and the 808 hip hop track has replaced the acoustic guitar in the studio. But for those seeking the days of Waylon and Willie, of turquoise buckles and bejeweled sports coats, and most important, of three chords and the truth, there is one remaining legit juke-joint, smoke-stained, wood-paneled dive bar in town that will take you back in time: Bobby's Idle Hour, right on 16th Avenue. Touted as "The Only Live Music Venue on Music Row," it might just be the last refuge for hit songwriters and industry veterans who remember Nashville a little differently than its current state.

Originally just a few doors up the road, Bobby's has been at its current location since 2004, and thanks to owner Lizard Thom Case, the character of the original came with it, carrying all of the memories and the mojo in the photographs and decorations that cover the interior. In its heyday, Bobby's was compared with Hollywood, with names like Kris Kristofferson, Billy Joe Shaver, Waylon Jennings, and Shel Silverstein being regulars, but also having bar tabs for Kenny Chesney and Toby Keith some years later. Stories of a fabled yellow parrot that lived in the bar for nearly twenty years are fading and the Styrofoam mascot in front of the Idle Hour has long since given up the ghost. But Bobby's has become that throwback retro kind of "hip" that is attracting a new generation of young talent who can be seen nightly

THE LAST LIVE MUSIC ON MUSIC ROW

WHAT Bobby's Idle Hour

WHERE 1028 Music Square E.

COST Free to enter

PRO TIP Check Google for their hours—at last check, they were Monday & Tuesday 4 p.m.– 1 a.m., Wednesday through Saturday noon-3 a.m., and Sunday noon to midnight.

Top: Bobby's wall of history
Inset: Bobby's welcoming exterior

up on stage, trying out their potential next big hit and taking advantage of the $2.50 beer. This is the one last tavern from the "glory days" standing on Music Row, so kindly pay your respects to this hidden gem before it's overwhelmed by progress.

Bobby's even has stand-up comedy nights for all the funny people out there.

12 BOY SCOUT CATFISH

What's the story with that catfish down on the corner?

Much like the random guitars of the GuitarTown Project and the artsy bike rack monuments, there are a number of out-of-place and doubletake-inducing catfish sculptures throughout town. The most memorable of these is the one schooling along in front of the Boy Scouts headquarters in Green Hills, outfitted in full Scout attire of green pants, a merit badge sash, the scout campaign hat, and catfish whiskers. As with any fish-in-a-costume sighting on a street corner, far more questions than answers come to mind.

The truth is simple: this is just one of around 51 art pieces, with names like *Bat Cat*, *Educat*, and *Spider Cat*, from the "Catfish Out of Water" project that benefitted the Cumberland River Compact, Greenways for Nashville, and the Parthenon Patrons Foundation in 2003, mainly to help clean the water of the Cumberland and bring awareness to the issue. Most of the fish were auctioned off to bidders and can be found in the front yards of private residences as well as business courtyards throughout town. A few of them, like *Be Prepared*, the Boy Scout catfish, can still be seen in public spaces, such as Centennial Park, Vanderbilt Children's Hospital, and the airport. Bidding is now, unfortunately, closed.

SOMETHING'S FISHY

WHAT The *Be Prepared* catfish sculpture

WHERE 3414 Hillsboro Pike

COST Free

PRO TIP Another fish that you can visit is on the northwest corner of Benton and Ridley.

Top: The Be Prepared *catfish*
Above left: A random fish sighting in Nashville
Above right: Northeast corner of Hillsboro and Woodmont

The Boy Scouts headquarters building is on the old site of Redoubt Two from the Civil War Battle of Nashville.

BRETT ELDREDGE SIGN

Where did Brett Eldredge have a #1?

In a more recent addition to Nashville's secret experiences, there is a random sign tucked back behind some bushes on the north side of the Warner Bros. Studios building on Music Row. You would think something like this would denote deep history where a Civil War battle happened or maybe where a significant Opry development took place . . . but nope. In actuality, this sign simply shows us where country star Brett Eldredge used to pee on his way to and from the bars.

Back in 2007, when Eldredge was a college student at Belmont, he and his buddies would walk to the bars after some pregame partying at the dorms and have to relieve themselves right around the time they got to the top of the Row. The massive Warner building was the perfect spot, with shadows and places to hide, so as not to get caught or arrested. The story was revealed to *People* magazine in a 2015 interview with Eldredge, and once his label caught wind of this, they decided to have some fun with his admission. When presenting Brett with a gold record for his album *Illinois* in June 2017, they immortalized his other "#1" activity with the plaque on the side of the building that simply says, "Brett Eldredge Left His Mark Here in March of 2007."

STREAMING HITS

WHAT Brett Eldredge marker

WHERE 20 Music Square E., north side of building

COST Free

PRO TIP If visiting in November, scope this same street on the night of the BMI Awards, where they roll out the red carpet for the arriving superstars.

Brett Eldredge's corner

BRETT ELDREDGE
LEFT HIS MARK HERE
IN MARCH *OF* 2007

This building is at Ground Zero for Music Row, steps away from the historical Quonset Hut and surrounding powerhouses of the industry.

14 CAPITOL GROUNDS

Who's buried in Polk's tomb?

Perched high on a downtown hill is the unmistakable Greek Revival architecture of the Tennessee State Capitol building, a National Historic Landmark completed in 1859. The building itself is worth a gander, but the surrounding grounds are where you'll find the good stuff, with plenty of historical Easter eggs around every bend.

First off, there are a lot of monuments—Presidents Johnson and Jackson, war heroes Sam Davis and Alvin York, and Senator Edward Ward Carmack. In addition, a memorial on the southwest corner of the grounds is a tribute to Africans who perished or survived the Middle Passage, when millions were shipped to the New World as part of the slave trade.

Most of the action is in the East Garden: a one-hundred-year time capsule buried on the grounds and scheduled to be dug up in 2027; a replica of the Liberty Bell that each state received in 1950 promoting the Korean War bond drive; six cedar trees serving as a Holocaust Memorial, dedicated to the Jewish victims of the Holocaust; and the survey marker that determines the height above sea level for the area. There's also a plaque commemorating the seventy-fifth anniversary of the United Daughters of the Confederacy, which was founded in Nashville.

And then there are the tombs, the first being that of architect William Strickland, who died before the building was completed; he is buried in the northern facade of the

GET YOUR STEPS IN

WHAT The East Garden of the Capitol

WHERE 600 Charlotte Ave.

COST The grounds are free, as are the Capitol tours offered daily every hour starting at 9 a.m.

PRO TIP The view from the northern end is one of the best in the city

Top left: Tennessee's own Liberty Bell replica
Top right: The tomb of President James Polk
Above left: The fountain near the Geodesic Survey Marker

building that is considered his greatest achievement. The other grave is the main draw of the hill: President James Polk and his wife, Sarah, both entombed in the East Garden. There has been a controversial motion to move the remains down to Columbia to a Polk family farm and museum, but no action has been taken as of this printing.

Originally on the site was the Holy Rosary Cathedral, the first Catholic Church in Tennessee, built back in 1820 but later torn down to make way for the Capitol.

<u>15</u> CASTELL GWYNN

Is that a legit castle floating in the clouds near Arrington?

South of Nashville, on a quick stretch of the I-840 bypass, is one of the most bewildering sights in the entire city: perched high up on a hill, growing larger with every passing white stripe of highway, is what appears to be a towering white medieval castle. The good news is that you're not seeing things—it is indeed a castle and is one of the coolest and most unique experiences in the area.

What you are seeing is Castell Gwynn—or "White Castle" and is the private home and lifelong dream of Mike Freeman (along with his wife, Jackie) ever since he was inspired by his high school architecture class in 1970. The first tower was built in 1980, the second in 1985, and the rest of the structure has been pieced together through the years. While the idea of a castle itself isn't too far-fetched in today's architecture, it's the details that lift this structure above and beyond, such as the 14,000 bricks in the archways of the kitchen, the twenty-eight-foot vaulted ceilings, giant fireplaces big enough to roast a cow in, copper-capped rooftops on the towers, and a collection of royal tapestries donated by Imogene Stone.

The best news of all? You can go visit Castell gwynn during the Tennessee Renaissance Festival that takes place every May! A tour of the castle is included in your admission price, and you'll also get to experience Nashville at its medieval-est.

GOING MEDIEVAL

WHAT Castell gwynn

WHERE 2124 New Castle Road, Arrington TN

COST Adults: $23.95, Children: $11.95

PRO TIP Make sure you get a turkey leg.

Top: The castle's interior brick archwork
Inset: Castell Gwynn

The festival even offers "theme weekends," from pirate invasions to Celtic attire.

16 CATFISH ON THE ICE

Why are there catfish on the hockey ice?

If you hang around Nashville for a few hours, it's easy to get a sense of our sports pride between the Tennessee Titans football team and our newest obsession, Nashville Predators Hockey. When the Predators take the ice at Bridgestone Arena, the home games are the loudest spot in town, with 19,000-plus fans in full-scream mode and a buzzing anticipation for Tim McGraw's altered version of "I Like It, I Love It" to reflect "I don't know what it is about those Predators scoring but I like it, I love it, I want some more of it."

A more questionable sight, though, is the number of real, no-bull catfish that appear on the ice throughout the game. During a big game, a playoff run, or a low period needing a boost, there's always a number of the slimy, whiskered Siluriformes (had to look that one up) sliding across the rink at some point in the game. So why in the world is this happening?

The practice dates back to 1998, when some fans wanted to retaliate against the visiting Detroit Red Wings and their fans' habit of throwing octopuses on the ice as a tradition. According to Bob Wolf, the former owner of Wolfy's bar, right across the street from Bridgestone, he was the first catfish-tosser, having gotten the idea from looking at the Cumberland River and trying to think of something memorable but safe they could throw into the action. Catfish came to mind and, much to the dismay of the arena, which doesn't technically permit the practice, they've been tossed on the ice for over twenty years now.

Also of note, there is a battle motto, "Instrument of Crime," which is what fan (and now local legend) Jake Waddell was hilariously charged with by Pittsburgh police when he threw a fish into the game at the Preds/Penguins Stanley Cup finals in 2017.

*Top: Catfish tank in Bridgestone Arena
Inset: A T-shirt tribute to the catfish
phenomenon from Project 615*

INSTRUMENT OF CRIME

WHAT Catfish thrown on the ice rink

WHERE 501 Broadway

COST Market price of catfish

PRO TIP The catfish must be smuggled in: wrap the fish in plastic wrap to keep the juices from seeping and then strap it to your back with more plastic wrap or a sports bandage.

There is actually a catfish tank inside Bridgestone, where you can take a selfie or two.

17 CAVE SPRING GROTTO

Does Shelby Park have any secrets?

Nashville has its share of hidden caves and springs, but here's one whose intrigue lies in the rumors that have been buried and forgotten over time. This forgotten wonder, which has most likely slipped the minds of most Nashville natives, is the Cave Spring grotto in East Nashville.

Just over the hill from the tennis courts and down the sloping hill in Shelby Park is a concrete altar of sorts, complete with crumbling stairs and columns, that looks like it has no earthly business being in the place it is. Actually, the grotto houses a natural spring that trickles year-round from a small subterranean cave but really comes to life and rolls down the cement chute toward nearby Sevier Lake if there is a heavy enough rain. The mysterious site used to be part of a turn-of-the-twentieth-century amusement park, surrounded by roller coasters, boat rides, and horseback riding trails until the developer went bankrupt in 1903. Shelby Park, as we now know it, opened to the public in 1912. The grotto is only ruins now, one of the unfortunate casualties of neglect and another potential reminder that for every skyscraper that goes up, a certain piece of Nashville history and culture is lost for the ages.

HOPE SPRINGS ETERNAL

WHAT Cave Spring Grotto

WHERE 401 S 20th St., down the hill behind the tennis courts

COST Free

PRO TIP Park in the lower parking lot just to the east of the tennis courts.

Top: The grotto in Shelby Park
Inset: Inside the spring

The grotto is adjacent to a dog park, so bring your pup along.

CELEBRITY HOUSE CLUSTER

So I've got, like, twenty minutes—where can I see some celebrity homes?

In a city like Nashville, where celebrities of all industries flock for the relaxed atmosphere and anonymity, it's pretty easy to find a famous home or two if you know where to look: like John Rich's "Mt. Richmore" on Love Circle, or Little Richard's penthouse suite behind the seven windows at the top of the Hilton downtown. But if you want the densest collection of celebrity houses in town, you'll want to head about five miles south of downtown on 8th Ave/Franklin Pike to Curtiswood Circle.

This loop of star-gazing starts with Martina McBride's house at 4409 Franklin Pike before turning onto Curtiswood Lane South, where Tex Ritter's house (which also makes it where John Ritter, the actor, grew up) will be on the left at 899 Curtiswood Lane South. Continuing on down, you will not be able to miss the Governor's Mansion on the right, at 882 Curtiswood Lane South, and that of previous neighbor Matthew Followill of the band Kings of Leon, at 874 Curtiswood Lane South (former house of Minnie Pearl). Just down the road on the left, there will be a white colonial a bit off the road at 851 Curtiswood. This is owned by Nashville native Reese Witherspoon, although not her primary residence. At this point, turn onto Curtiswood Lane North and head up to 806, which is Ronnie Milsap's house and the former residence of Ray Stevens, where he lived when he got into his spat with Webb Pierce. Right across the street is the bus pull-in for Webb's old residence at 4401 Franklin Pike. This is the house with the guitar-shaped pool and the very driveway where fans would flock to hang with Webb and aggravate Mr. Stevens back in the day.

Top: A Witherspoon property
Above left: Governor's mansion

HOMES OF STARS

WHAT Nashville's densest cluster

WHERE Curtiswood Lane North and South

COST Free

PRO TIP There are several other celebrity homes surrounding this general area, many featured in the book and app, *Now You Know Nashville*.

This street is the heart of Civil War history, right on the Battle of Nashville battlefield.

CENTENNIAL PARK TRAIN

Why is there a train sitting in the middle of Centennial Park?

Spend enough time in Nashville and you'll eventually wind up at Centennial Park. Spend enough time at Centennial Park and you'll eventually wind up walking over to the full-size locomotive engine on the west side and saying, "What in God's name is this doing here?" Considered a living piece of Nashville history, this particular engine is the Nashville, Chattanooga, and St. Louis No 576, one of the last steam engines built in the country and designed to haul soldiers and oil during World War II. It was donated to Metro Parks by the railroad back in 1952 and has been sitting in this spot for decades.

However, the story does not end there, and you should move quickly to see the engine in this spot while you can: approval was given in 2016 to restore the locomotive back to working condition and have it be an active engine in the Music City Star fleet that transports travelers between Mt. Juliet and downtown. Fundraising and restoration will take a number of years, but it will be a step in the right direction to have a piece of Nashville history back in action rather than left to deteriorate.

An interactive sign at the display tells the history of the Nashville & Chattanooga Railroad.

TRAIN OF THOUGHT MOVING CO.

WHAT Engine in Centennial Park

WHERE Centennial Park: 27th Ave N., near Park and 31st

COST Free

PRO TIP It's a two-minute walk to the lake and gardens of the park, just east of the train.

The Centennial Park train

The tracks in front of the train are a popular spot to lie down and "plank" for a remarkable pic.

20 CHATEAU ON THE ROW

Is there anywhere to stay right on Music Row?

If a visitor wants a truly unique Nashville experience, why not stay and sleep in a fully functioning recording studio? This can be done at Chateau on the Row, a truly "only in Nashville" kind of experience and a legit vacation rental located in the upper loft of Jay's Place, a 17th Avenue tracking room that has recorded the likes of Chet Atkins, Dobie Grey, Trisha Yearwood, and Garth Brooks. Jay himself is Jay Vernali, a piano virtuoso who has played with, recorded, and/or produced Keith Whitley, Eddie Rabbitt, Dobie Gray, Lee Greenwood, the Funk Brothers, and countless more.

The Chateau's one-bedroom apartment is appropriately music-themed in its décor and also allows guests to witness the studio in operation, perhaps recording the next hit record right below their feet. The music dies down long before evening, though, so there's plenty of peace and quiet to be had when it's bedtime. Guests even get a personal tour of the studio from the owners. The location is right on 17th Avenue, a prime location for walking the Row, hitting Bobby's Idle Hour, and exploring Midtown.

Reviews and booking information can be found through your favorite vacation rental sites or by simply emailing Jay himself: jaysplacerecording@comcast.net

AIR R&B

WHAT Only B&B in a studio

WHERE 1508 17th Ave S.

COST Rates vary by season—contact jaysplacerecording@comcast.net

PRO TIP Don't be shy about experiencing the studio—it's a very rare opportunity.

Top: Jay's Place Recording Studio
Inset: Inside Jay's Place.
Photo courtesy of Chateau on the Row.

At one recent recording session, the musicians had played on albums that had sold over 650 million combined copies.

21 CHET ATKINS STATUE

Want to have a beer with the one of the greatest guitar players ever?

Nashville does not have an open container policy, so it's still illegal to have a drink on the downtown streets, but that doesn't stop the statue of Chet Atkins on the northeast corner of Fifth Avenue and Union from collecting a can or three over the course of the night. The unique statue, unveiled in June of 2001 and designed by sculptor Russell Faxon, features the guitar virtuoso in mid-pickin' form while an empty stool sits adjacent, waiting for the next guest to sit in on the jam session. This was a common occurrence for Atkins while he was alive, having produced and rocked it out with thousands of players and artists (such as Roy Orbison, the Everly Brothers, Dolly Parton, and Perry Como) during his career, which spanned the decades from the 1940s to the '90s, and for which he was credited as the creator of the "Nashville Sound."

Bank of America commissioned the corner monument, which was one of the first tributes to country music featured downtown. Intended for an opportune photo moment, the bronze statue has become a popular place for passersby to take a load off, grab a photo, and tip on back a secret stashed cold one with the legend.

Half a block away are the Arcade and historical Woolworth on 5th.

Chet's Corner

JAM WITH CHET

WHAT Chet Atkins Corner

WHERE Northeast corner of 5th Ave. N and Union

COST Free

PRO TIP Have a friend take your pic on the adjacent stool.

CHRISTIE COOKIE

Where can I get free famous cookies?

This one had you at "free cookie"! Plus, as an added bonus, it might even be the world-famous cookie that only comes with your check-in at a hotel that features two trees. Right here in Nashville, nestled in East Germantown, is the factory for the Christie Cookie Company, featured on *How It's Made* and *Unwrapped,* and perhaps most important, it's the official baker of the revered Doubletree Cookie. There are, unfortunately, no tours offered of the factory itself; however, if you go in the lobby at just the right time (when the "Fresh Cookies" sign is glowing in neon), raid the freezer and purchase a tub of some killer chocolate chip/peanut butter/southern pecan/100 percent butter cookie dough, you might also be offered a free cookie for stopping in.

The first Christie Cookie store was opened on Church Street in 1985 by Christie Hauck, a gentleman who also jumped into the gelato world shortly after with the Bravo Gelato brand. The cookie company made a few moves and finally ended up in Germantown at its current facility. Not many locals are aware that this world-renowned factory is right around the corner, so you'd best beat the crowds before word gets around.

New locations are popping up all over town, and their sweet treats can be found at dozens of local restaurants. Check out their website and cookie options at www.ChristieCookies.com.

A number of flavors are available as raw dough in a tub.

What's on today's menu

IT'S COOKIE TIME!

WHAT Christie Cookie Co

WHERE 1205 3rd Ave N.

COST Goods and prices vary;
Hours: M-F 8 am-4 pm, Sat 9
am-3 pm

PRO TIP Grab a burger across
the street at Jack Brown's Beer
and Burger Joint.

23 CIVIL WAR EARTHWORKS

Are there any remnants from the Civil War visible around Green Hills?

Long ago, in 1864, as the Battle of Nashville was unfolding for control of the area and river access, Confederate forces advanced and retreated while Union soldiers held their posts and battled back, each side using any means necessary to fortify its position. This included shoveling large mounds and trenches into a feature called an earthwork, which is pretty much an organized pile of dirt that creates an embankment and, using nothing but soil, provides the best coverage possible during a battle. There are many earthworks all around Middle Tennessee, most of which are now stealthily hidden beneath the underbrush or smoothed out to where they are barely noticeable.

One earthwork that remains intact is located on Woodmont Boulevard right in the heart of Green Hills, integrating itself into the landscape of this private residence. This marks part of General Hood's Confederate line, where the soldiers camped while waiting for the weather to clear and at one time included a more official site, named Redoubt Two, until housing developments destroyed it in the 1990s; the only signs left are in this location. The swells and falls of the grass are well-manicured, making it difficult to ever imagine the horrors of war ravaging this same earth . . . but once upon a time, trees were uprooted, bullets grazed the ground, and blood spilled across this same dust.

THE HILLS ARE ALIVE

WHAT Redoubt Two remnants

WHERE 1811 Woodmont

COST Free

PRO TIP Don't actually walk on the lawn or you might get arrested.

The subtle swells of Civil War earthworks

Many other historical monuments and redoubts are scattered throughout the Nashville area, and it's not hard to find them, but this earthwork in particular has remained a more hidden local secret.

Redoubt One is walking distance away at 3421 Benham Avenue.

24 COOTER'S PLACE

Is Hazzard County anywhere near Nashville?

This isn't a terribly well-kept secret, as it's in brochures and advertisements all around town. However, it's not always a top priority on visitors' to-do lists but probably should be once they see what they could be missing. Right in the heart of the Opry Drive complex is a museum called Cooter's Place, dedicated to the pop culture phenomenon film and TV show *The Dukes Of Hazzard*, and it's owned and operated by one of the show's main stars, Mr. Ben Jones, who played the Dukes' mechanic and partner in crime, "Cooter."

For the hopeful, yes, there are a number of General Lee cars featured, as well as Daisy's Jeep, Rosco P. Coltrane's (you just said that in your head, didn't you?) squad car, Cooter's tow truck, and thousands of items from the filming and societal impact of the show. If you're really lucky, you might even pop into Cooter's when there's a Dukes convention going on, where Tom Wopat, John Schneider, and Catherine Bach, among others, are known to stop by. The best news: the museum is free! It does cost a few bucks to get your picture taken with the cars, though, but what's a fiver in exchange for being behind the wheel of the General Lee, jumping a cop car, and screaming, "Yeeeeeee hawwwww!"

A few doors down is the Caney Fork Restaurant, where Randy Travis was discovered while washing dishes, back when it was the Nashville Palace.

Top: Cooter's collection
Above: The General Lee

DUKES OF HAZZARD HEAVEN

WHAT Cooter's Place

WHERE 2613 McGavock Pike

COST Free to enter; $5 for a photo inside the cars on display

PRO TIP Check www.CootersPlace.com to see if any Dukes stars are signing autographs

25 COUNTRY MUSIC HALL OF FAME DESIGN

Why does that building look so weird?

The interior design and the exhibits in the Country Music Hall of Fame are the main reasons that folks head to the building with mind-blowing artifacts, instruments, original lyric sheets, and costumes galore. However, the structure also holds its own secrets and fascination with some hidden tributes in its exterior architecture, assuming you know where to look.

The design is the work of famed architect Ralph Applebaum, known for his work with the William J. Clinton Presidential Library and the Newseum in Washington, D.C., among many others. Applebaum wanted an edifice that reflected the lifestyles of country music listeners, so he incorporated a number of those elements into the project, the most visible and recognizable one being the piano keys that make up the windows of the main facade, with two black keys and three white keys repeating their pattern as the wave swells from left to right, like a loose leaf of sheet music. Some have claimed the swell also looks like the fin of a '59 Cadillac.

COUNTRY BY DESIGN

WHAT Country Music Hall of Fame

WHERE 222 5th Ave S.

COST Tickets start at $27.95 but exterior views are free.

PRO TIP Make SURE you take the RCA B Studio tour!

Note the ornamental owls in the trees outside, watching over the crowds and keeping the real birds at bay.

Left: The Hall Of Fame rotunda
Right: The curious architecture of the Country Music Hall of Fame

The rotunda is a competing eye-catcher, with a replica of the upper portion of the WSM antenna capping the top, sitting on top of a stack of disc media, from a compact disc to a 45 to an LP vinyl record and finally a 78. The rotunda shape itself is reminiscent of a grain silo or even a water tower, echoing the common sights within the southern (and essentially all) farming communities. The building materials that make up the rotunda are native to the mid-South, such as local wood and concrete, Crab Orchard stone from East Tennessee, and steel beams paying tribute to the rail history of the area. The stone inlays circling the outside of the rotunda are the notated melody for the gospel/rockabilly classic "Will the Circle Be Unbroken," complete with treble staff lines circling the cylinder. Finally, a very tough-to-see design element is that the outline of the building looks like a giant bass clef when viewed from above—something to keep your eye out for on your flight in or out.

The interior is another level of detail, with the grand staircase showing similarities to the rivers and waterfalls of the Middle Tennessee area, each floor having its own theme and motif related to show business, and details within the Hall of Fame displays in the rotunda interior. But those are secrets for another day.

CURSE OF THE GRAND OLE OPRY

Is the Opry cursed?

A little research into the growing list of Grand Ole Opry members clearly shows that many of them have died tragic and horrible deaths. A number have been victims of plane crashes, like Patsy Cline and Jim Reeves; others were murdered, like Stringbean Akeman. The automobile has played a factor in a number of other Opry-related deaths, such as those of Dottie West, Billy Walker, and Ira Louvin while the voices of Hank Williams and Jack Greene were almost silenced in critical crashes. Recently, the late Jean Shepard's husband was stabbed and nearly murdered at their home during a break-in, and other Nashville celebrities have succumbed to drug and alcohol abuse or even fires (Texas Ruby Fox). Now, many members are perfectly fine and will continue to be so, while others have passed away in a perfectly natural manner, but for those whose ends were more macabre, there is a growing legend known as the "Curse of the Grand Ole Opry."

There is no known beginning to the Curse, but it's been attributed to not only a number of deaths of stars but also to the accidents and deaths of visitors to the new Opryland complex: 14 alone in the three-year span after the show moved to the new Opry House in '74. The Ryman is also a large part of the legend (as another section in this book has detailed), with the ghosts of Hank, Patsy, and the Grey Man said to still walk its halls and sit in the pews.

The Opry House itself is not known to be haunted . . . yet.

Top: The Opry House exterior
Inset: The stage of the Grand Ole Opry

OH, CURSES . . .

WHAT Curse of the Grand Ole Opry

WHERE The Opry, Opryland, Opry Mills

COST Free

PRO TIP Keep your head up!

27 DEMONBREUN'S CAVE

Where did the first Caucasian resident of Nashville live?

If you roam the streets of Nashville, you will soon notice a not-too-easy-to-pronounce word popping up on street signs and historical markers: Demonbreun. Go ahead—try to say it and start getting used to second guessing the pronunciation (duh-MUN-bree-un). What's up with this word? Well, it's the name of a French-Canadian fur trader, Timothy Demonbreun (anglicized from Jacques-Timothée Boucher, Sieur de Montbrun), who stumbled upon this area of the Cumberland River and decided to set up camp due to the abundance of wildlife drawn to the nearby salt lick. Trouble was, he didn't have a permanent shelter, and there were more than a few natives who were out to get Demonbreun, so he needed a place to hide out for a bit. Lucky for him, a natural cave in the river bend provided a relatively easy location in which to hang his coonskin hat, just a mile up the river from the spring and accessible by boat. This essentially became the first residence of a non-native in the area. And it worked well for a few months until he was able to set up shop for many years as a tavern keeper, merchant, and fur trader.

View the cave and keep your feet dry by taking the *General Jackson* showboat or straying off the bike trails of Shelby Bottoms Park.

Left: Demonbreun's cave from afar
Right: A look inside the cave

The cave, now part of the local drainage system, is accessible by water or by an extremely precarious rock shimmy, so pack your kayak and be ready to paddle a few yards west on the Cumberland River from the launch point off River Hills Drive. A steel grate has protected the cave (and you) for a number of years but was damaged in the 2010 flood, so you can still pop in for the time being and pretend you're a fur-trading pioneer hiding out from the locals.

NASHVILLE'S FIRST HOUSE

WHAT Demonbreun's cave

WHERE Approximately 1707 River Hills Dr., across the street and down on the riverbank

COST Free

PRO TIP This is a very slippery and challenging site, so USE EXTREME CAUTION!

28 DEMONBREUN'S GRAVE

Where is Timothy Demonbreun buried?

This is one of the most persistent questions in Nashville lore: what happened to the bones of the first Nashville native, Mr. Timothy Demonbreun? We know that he settled in the area after his arrival in 1766 and that he became a prominent trader in the region as the city developed, complete with a storefront and a tavern on the public square. We even know that he lived at 3rd Avenue and Broadway, and that he died at this home in October 1826. The big question is: what happened to the body of this revered man?

Assumptions are that he ended up either buried north of town in the backyard of the John Geist and Sons Blacksmith Shop or in the City Cemetery, the latter being the more likely of the two based on his stature in the community. However, no records can be found that date back that far, and no confirmed remains have ever been identified as his. There are statues of Demonbreun (check out the 1st Avenue one on the banks of the Cumberland), a major street is named after him, and there are even memorials to him in far-off Ashland City, but his burial spot has been lost to time and is one of Nashville's forgotten secrets, at least for the time being.

The blacksmith shop opened in 1886 and was the city's oldest business in continuous family ownership and operation when it closed in 2006.

Top: Nashville City Cemetery
Inset: Geist and Sons courtyard

THE FIRST AND FINAL

WHAT Demonbreun's grave

WHERE City Cemetery at 1001 4th Ave S? Geist and Sons at 311 Jefferson St?

COST Free

PRO TIP While looking around for Monsieur Demonbreun, pay your respects to Harlan Howard, Music Row's godfather of songwriters, who's buried in the City Cemetery.

29

DOOR TO NOWHERE

Where does that door way up there go?

The RCA Studio A building has received a lot of attention lately, coming close to demolition before gaining National Register of Historic Places status. Music Row legends Chet Atkins and the Bradley brothers originally opened this studio in 1964, and Ben Folds was a recent resident producer for twelve years up, until 2014 when Dave Cobb took over. The recording studio has produced a number of phenomenal albums by the likes of Chris Stapleton, Kacey Musgraves, and Sturgill Simpson, and has a storied history with artists like Dolly Parton, Willie Nelson, and Charlie Pride.

Legacy aside, a good look at the back of the building will present an intriguing question: why is there a door halfway up the side of the wall? There is no balcony, no railing, no explanation as to what it's doing there or who in their right mind would step through it. Inside, the door is simply like any other door on the 3rd floor, speculated to have been used to move furniture and perhaps recording equipment in and out of the building in its early days. Outside, its precarious position offers more questions than answers.

In a case of strange but true folk lore, it actually has been used and, at one time, went somewhere—in an example of the lengths publishers will go to in order to find success. Story goes that in the '70s, Bill Hall (of Jack and Bill Publishing) had a song called "Running Bear" that he felt would be perfect for an artist (most likely Sonny James) whom Jerry Bradley, the head of RCA Records at the time (and Owen's son), had on his label. Jerry's third floor office in Studio A was apparently a

The door to nowhere actually leads somewhere every once in a while.

The rear view of RCA A and the floating "door to nowhere"

WATCH YOUR STEP!

WHAT RCA Studio A third floor door

WHERE 30 Music Square W., in the back parking lot

COST Free to look at the exterior

PRO TIP No tours are offered, so if you find yourself inside, consider yourself very blessed.

little hard to reach, but Bill really, really wanted to get him this one particular song. So, given the circumstances, the most sensical solution to Bill was to rent a cherry picker, rise up to the door, and have Jerry receive his musical gift. Lo and behold, Jerry did answer the door himself, received the tape, bid Bill adieu, and actually ended up recording "Running Bear."

30

EGYPTIAN TEMPLE

What wonders await behind those temple doors?

The Downtown Presbyterian Church on this Nashville city street corner has seen its share of high times since its initial construction in 1814, like when Andrew Jackson was presented a ceremonial sword on its steps after the Battle of New Orleans in 1815, as well as when James Polk held his inauguration as the Governor of Tennessee there in 1939. It's also had its share of hard times, having burned to the ground in 1832 and again in 1848. However, there may have been a higher power involved, as subsequent renovations and the current design by William Strickland, who also had a hand in the Tennessee State Capitol building, are regarded as examples of the best- preserved Egyptian Revival architecture in the United States.

A step into the fascinating sanctuary reveals the motif of an Egyptian temple, modeled after the temple of Karnak, complete with columns and symbols, bright colors and perspectives, serpents, and a repeating motif of the sun god Amun-Ra splashed throughout the décor. Other items of note within the structure are the curved bench pews reminiscent of the Ryman with name plates featuring a Who's Who of Nashville historical figures, appropriate church-style stained glass, and a 4,000-pound bell donated by Adelicia Acklen hanging in the western bell tower.

INSIDE JOB

WHAT Downtown Presbyterian Church

WHERE 154 5th Ave N.

COST Free (donations appreciated) but tours need to be set up in advance

PRO TIP Check out the Vinyl Bunker in the adjacent parking garage for an eclectic and truly underground record haven.

Top: The interior Egyptian decor
Inset: Downtown Presbyterian Church

Throughout its history, the building has served as a military hospital in the Civil War, a flood refuge, and a community shelter. Today, the National Historic Landmark church has a motto of "Where you are welcome. No exceptions" and is open to the public for their 11 a.m. Sunday worship.

The members purchased the church in 1954 to save it from demolition.

31 ELVIS STATUE

Can I get a selfie with that Elvis statue that's always on TV?

One of the most photographed spots in Music City, other than the Parthenon, might just be with the King of Rock 'n' Roll standing guard outside of Legends Gifts on Broadway and also Nashville Limited on 2nd Ave. These are pretty identical Elvises (or "Elvi"?), so take your pick on the photo op—but the one outside of Legend's is probably the one that ends up on most posts and would be the one that I'd pick, given the choice.

Contrary to popular opinion, and despite being mere feet from the Ryman, Elvis only played the Grand Ole Opry one time, on Oct 2, 1954, with a performance, shall we say, very "ahead of its time," after which the talent manager, Jim Denny, asked Elvis if he still had the keys to the truck he used to drive for his day job. Luckily, the Louisiana Hayride residency followed shortly thereafter and allowed the world a little more time to grow into Elvis's style.

As far as the statues go, they're purely a gimmick to make us stop and stare. There's no major historical affiliation to Elvis in this part of town or at these venues. It's just something to make you check out the souvenir shop that just happens to make it on every Food Network segment about Nashville.

ELVIS HAS LEFT THE BUILDING

WHAT Elvis statue

WHERE 424 Broadway

COST Free

PRO TIP In the stores, the policy is: "You break it, you buy it."

An Elvis sighting downtown

There is yet another Elvis statue at 4900 Charlotte Pike, outside of Cool Stuff Weird Things.

32 FIRES OF DYER

Has Nashville ever had any witches?

That's a very strange and random question to ask, but actually, Nashville indeed has a history of witch-hunting and subsequent haunting by the wrongly accused. A little south of Nashville, down in Rutherford County near the town of Windrow, legend says that three women were accused of witchcraft, went on the run, and were eventually cornered in a wooded area, where they were captured, hung, and their bodies burned. They were buried where they were killed, right there in the area where the cemetery stands today.

Today, there are terrifying whispers of the paranormal: gates fly open with no help, shadowy figures are seen in the southeast corner, and voices or footsteps are heard on the wind. Toward the front of the cemetery, a certain tree is supposedly the exact one where the women were hanged, near which people are said to have felt phantom fingernails on their skin. And the strangest phenomena are balls of fire that have been seen floating toward the tree before rising up into the branches and disappearing.

The isolation here is unnerving, and if you decide to experience the Fires of Dyer yourself, you will be on your own and getting a good feel for the same terror the women felt in their final moments.

The majority of names on the gravestones in the cemetery are from the Dyer family, as well as the Leathers family, which care for the cemetery today.

Dyer Cemetery

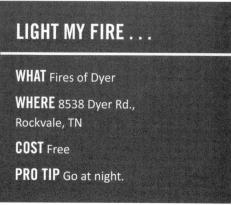

LIGHT MY FIRE . . .

WHAT Fires of Dyer

WHERE 8538 Dyer Rd., Rockvale, TN

COST Free

PRO TIP Go at night.

33 FOUNDING OF THE KKK

Why was the KKK founded in Middle Tennessee?

All right, let's get through this one quickly. We're not very proud of this fact, but the truth is out there so we might as well face it. Yes, the Ku Klux Klan was indeed started in Middle Tennessee, south of Nashville in a small town named Pulaski, and it has been making the world a lesser place ever since. In 1865, a few veterans of the Confederacy decided to get together and form this secret fraternity as a social group but quickly got caught up in the tumultuous times of the Reconstructionist South, escalating to a more violent group—dead-set on minimizing the rights of the newly freed African Americans. And let the hopeful truth be told again: the KKK's first grand wizard, Nathan Bedford Forrest (more on him later), allegedly attempted to disband the group after the violence grew out of control but was obviously unsuccessful at doing so.

The Klan has experienced ebbs and flows in its membership, but it's collectively agreed by the rest of us that its eradication cannot come soon enough. For the truly curious, an hour's drive down I-65 will take you to Pulaski, where, on Madison Street, you can find a historical marker at the location of the initial fraternity's meetings. It has since been turned around by the building's owners and is now unreadable.

Around the corner is the Sam Davis Museum, built on the spot where the Confederate "Boy Hero" was hung as a spy by Union forces.

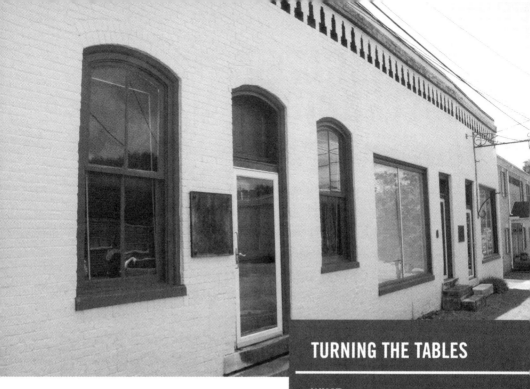

A site of infamy

TURNING THE TABLES

WHAT Where the KKK was founded

WHERE 205 W. Madison St., Pulaski, TN

COST Free

PRO TIP Use the Natchez Trace as a route for this journey to take the longer, more scenic way.

34 FULL-SCALE MILLENNIUM FALCON

Can Chewy get us out of here?

A newfound rumor around the Nashville sci-fi underground is the construction of a full-size Millennium Falcon, of *Star Wars* fame, somewhere in the vicinity of the city. In 2005, Chris Lee of Nashville launched his ambitious campaign to replicate the 114-foot hunk of space junk known as Corellian model YT-1300 in full detail with a down-to-the-button cockpit, blaster pod, walkable hallways, and a fully functional hyperdrive mode (OK, that last one might be a few millennia away). Wisely, Mr. Lee has enlisted the help of fans all over the United States, from Pennsylvania to Texas to California, to build certain sections of the Falcon, and at the right point in the future, piece them all together to form the entire ship, a la Voltron. Construction began in 2010 and is commencing countdown as interest for the project gains momentum. New progress is made every month, and it's only a matter of time before the ship is looming on the horizon. As of now, there are no tours, and the location is very private; Nashville and its legion of *Star Wars* fans are left patiently waiting for this promised new wonder of the galaxy to land nearby.

NOT SO LONG AGO, IN A GALAXY RIGHT HERE . . .

WHAT Full-Scale Falcon Project

WHERE Unknown

COST N/A

PRO TIP "Don't get cocky, kid!"

Top: Unofficial Falcon schematics. Photo courtesy of Stinson Lenz, Full-Scale Falcon Project.
Inset: The project awakens. Photo courtesy of Chris Lee, Full-Scale Falcon Project.

Designs are based on the movie sets, but all blueprints and models are to be created by the Project.

35 GARTH BROOKS MET TRISHA YEARWOOD

So how did Garth and Trisha hook up?

This is a tough one to give away since this is one of those secrets that even the most well-informed Nashville natives don't know. Tucked away in Green Hills, a few blocks away from the world-renowned Bluebird Café, sits a house like a lot of other houses on a street like a lot of other streets. But what makes this one stand out is what happened back in 1987 when songwriter Kent Blazy was doing a few homemade demos out of this house and got introduced to a new kid in town named Garth Brooks. Kent used Garth's voice on a few demos and thought he'd pair up perfectly on a duet with another singer he frequently used, Trisha Yearwood. Yep, it was in this house that musical history was made: Garth and Trisha met, their voices merged in harmonic excellence, and Sandy, Garth's wife at the time, felt a great disturbance in the Force.

Also of note, this is the same house where Kent and Garth wrote a little ditty called "If Tomorrow Never Comes," which became Garth's first number one hit and launched the legendary phenomenon.

Remember: This is private property, so photos should be taken from the street only, folks.

THE DYNASTY BEGINS

WHAT The house where Garth met Trisha

WHERE 1705 Warfield Dr.

COST Free but no tours—private residence

PRO TIP See your favorite songwriters and aspiring artists just around the corner at the Bluebird Café.

Top: The house where it all began
Inset: Trisha and Garth hanging at Douglas Corner

Up-and-coming stars like Faith Hill, Doug Stone, Billy Dean, Joe Diffie, and Martina McBride also recorded demos at this house.

GATES TO STARDOM

What's the story with the Ryman gates?

The distance between the Ryman and Tootsies is pretty common knowledge thanks to Willie Nelson's famous claim that from the Ryman, it was "seventeen steps to Tootsies and thirty-four back." Along that alleyway, greats like Faron Young, Kris Kristofferson, Patsy Cline, Hank Williams, and hundreds more have walked . . . and stumbled . . . between two of the most famous locales in all of country music history.

But there's another, far less-well-known event that took place right in this same walkway. Back in the late '50s, a couple of boys would hang out playing a guitar and serenading the passing Opry stars as they made their way out the backstage door and over to their next destination (most likely Tootsies). They did this night after night, day after day, hanging out by that pathway of stars, singing their songs, tightening their harmonies, and trying to catch the ear of anyone passing by. And one day, they actually did catch an ear, when Chet Atkins passed by and said (paraphrasing), "Boys, y'all are starting to sound real good. Why don't you join me on the Opry tonight?" And history was written. Those boys became known as the Everly Brothers, and they were essentially discovered right on those backstage steps of the Ryman.

BACKSTAGE ACCESS

WHAT The Gates to Stardom

WHERE Alley between Ryman and Tootsies, second set of gated stairs

COST Free

PRO TIP The alley provides back door access to several Broadway joints

Top: Tootsie's Alley between the bar and the Ryman
Above left: 17 steps to Tootsie's
Above right: The backstage stairs of the Ryman

Point your eyes to the ground to see the inlaid footprints that represent the Ryman-to-Tootsies walk.

37 GHOSTS OF THE RYMAN

Who haunts the Ryman?

One of the most popular spots on any Nashville tour is the Ryman Auditorium, the Mother Church of Country Music. Its legacy in music history is cemented by its conversion from a tabernacle to the consistently voted "#1 Best Venue In America." If you get a chance to see a show there, GO! But only if you want to experience the best concert environment around today.

If you want to experience the supernatural, the Ryman might be a good bet for that as well. As with any historical building, there are the darker stories from the darker times of the Ryman, with claims being consistently made by security personnel about Patsy Cline's heels being heard echoing the halls in the dead of night. Hank Williams's ghost is said to frequent the stage, whispering in his unmistakable voice, shutting down power like he did to Bill Anderson in the middle of an ol' Hank tune, and also hanging around the back gate, reflecting on the times when he was banished from the venue. Even Thomas Ryman's ghost has been reported to disrupt more questionable shows that include themes that Ryman wouldn't have agreed with while he was alive.

THE CORNER OF YOUR EYE . . .

WHAT Ghosts of the Ryman

WHERE 116 5th Ave N.

COST Tickets starting at $21.95

PRO TIP Splurge for the guided backstage tour.

Minnie Pearl's original shoes and hat, along with its dangling price tag, are on display on the lower floor.

Top left: The towering Ryman facade
Top right: Pews of the lower level
Above left: Creepy staircases around every corner
Above right: Minnie's hat on display

And then there's the Grey Man in Section 13. In the upper balcony of the 1897 Confederate Gallery, when the house is empty and dark, a lonely soldier in grey can often be seen silhouetted against the wood pews in this section, in silent contemplation of a war-torn nation.

Ghosts or no ghosts, the Ryman is a spectacular venue, tour, and experience, and this author can't really blame these ghosts for still wanting to hang at their old haunt.

GRAND OLE OPRY CIRCLE

Where is THE most coveted spot to play in Nashville?

While there are plenty of places in Nashville that are steeped in history, like the Quonset Hut on 16th or the McNairy and Sulphur Springs, which are paramount locations to Music City, there's one spot where you can stand and be walking in the footsteps of hundreds of music legends: the stage of the Grand Ole Opry.

From 1943 to 1974, the Grand Ole Opry ran continuously from the stage of the Ryman Auditorium, where greats like Hank Williams, Willie Nelson, Patsy Cline, Dolly Parton, and many, many others performed their hits on the radio show. When the Grand Ole Opry House was completed in 1974 and the show moved across town, a six-foot circle was cut out of the rear stage-left portion of the Ryman stage, which was reputed to be where all of the stars stood waiting for their turn in the spotlight.

This circle is now front and center on the "new" Opry stage, right where the mic goes for today's artists and where today's legends—like Garth Brooks, Keith Urban, Miranda Lambert, and Zac Brown, to name a few—plant their feet to perform for their fans. You too can stand there when you take a backstage tour of the Grand Ole Opry.

Send fan mail to your favorite Opry Member at "(Artist Name), Grand Ole Opry, Nashville, TN 37214" and it will go right to their P.O. box at the Opry.

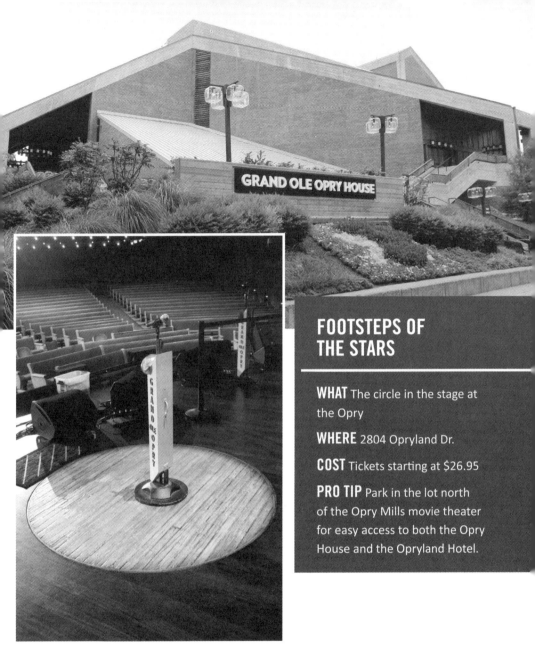

FOOTSTEPS OF
THE STARS

WHAT The circle in the stage at the Opry

WHERE 2804 Opryland Dr.

COST Tickets starting at $26.95

PRO TIP Park in the lot north of the Opry Mills movie theater for easy access to both the Opry House and the Opryland Hotel.

Top: The Grand Ole Opry House
Inset: The famous Circle

39 GRAVITY HILL

Going up? Or down . . .

Over on the southwest side of town is Edwin Warner Park, which holds a number of history's mysteries within its boundaries. One of the most popular of those enigmas is Gravity Hill, a strange road jutting off Old Hickory Blvd., where the laws of gravity are put to the test. Legend has it that if you put your car in neutral at the bottom of the hill, you will inexplicably roll UP the hill. Same goes for bicycles, water bottles, and soccer balls—they all roll uphill. Many of these mystery hills exist across the world, creating legend and speculation wherever they pop up—are they gravitational anomalies? Are they threatening vortices attempting to burst out of the ground like the Upside Down? And most important, do we have one right here in Middle Tennessee?!

All we know is that experiments have been done and scientific conclusions have been made, but it's far more fun to leave it up to you to decide on your own personal hypothesis. While there is now a gate blocking cars from accessing the hill, you can still test it with any rolling object and see it in action.

Nearby, you can see pop culture spots like the "Small World House" at 1644 Chickering and Reyna and Deacon's mansion from the show Nashville at 1358 Page Road.

Top: Gravity Hill
Inset: The "Small World" house

WHERE DOWN IS UP

WHAT Gravity Hill

WHERE Near Old Hickory Blvd. and Vaughn Road, a quarter mile northwest of Vaughn on the south side of the road, with a big gate guarding the entrance.

COST Free

PRO TIP Bring a larger item to experiment with, as smaller items don't catch enough momentum.

40 GUITAR-SHAPED POOLS

I've seen it on TV–where's the guitar-shaped swimming pool?

It's no secret that there are a number of swimming pools shaped like guitars peppered throughout Nashville, but the big secret is where these bad boys actually are. Chances are, if you've taken any tours of Nashville, you probably rode or walked right past a few of them without even knowing. The most conveniently located one is right at the head of Music Row, at the concrete monolith of Spence Manor. Unfortunately, the pool isn't just sitting there exposed, but you can get a good eyeful by peeking through the fence during your walk around the Row. Aside from having the pool, Spence Manor also has its own history as a former apartment occupied at one time or other by the Beatles, Willie Nelson, and Elvis, the sordid details of which shouldn't be exposed in a family-oriented book such as this.

So why the guitar shape? Well, the story for that goes back to the original guitar-shaped swimming pool, still dive-ready down at Webb Pierce's old place on Curtiswood Drive. Mr. Pierce owned the home in the '70s and happily catered to his adoring fans, who would congregate outside his house and wait for him to come sign autographs. They'd also peek through his fence and admire his pool, which was shaped like—you guessed it—a guitar. The attraction of Webb and his pool didn't thrill all the neighbors, though, most notably Ray

Other pools of similar shape have popped up at some local hotels and even at John Rich's home on Love Circle.

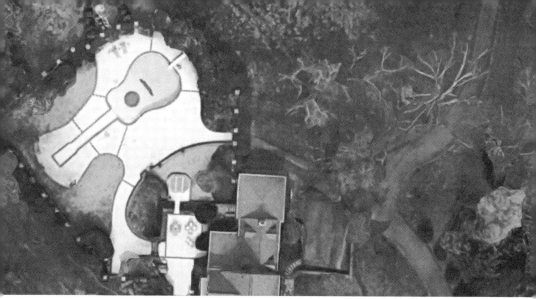

Top: Webb Pierce's original guitar-shaped pool from above. Photo courtesy of Google Maps.
Above: The pool at Spence Manor

Stevens, who filed numerous complaints for public nuisance from all the activity. In an effort to thin the masses, Webb contracted a new pool to be built near Music Row in hopes that the fans would flock to that pool instead, but that pool featured neither Webb nor his house, so it never made much of a splash.

41 HEART OF MUSIC ROW

Can you find it?

Right in the center of Music Row, the building housing Starstruck Entertainment is surrounded by a handcrafted brick wall. And it is here that a masonry craftsman had a novel idea during construction: to make "the heart of Music Row" a reality. Somewhere in this wall is a heart-shaped brick that once you see, you won't be able to un-see.

Starstruck Entertainment is the company founded in 1988 by country music legend Reba McEntire with her then-husband and manager, Narvel Blackstock. Since McEntire split from the company in 2016 to open up Reba's Business Inc., Narvel now owns the company, which focuses on writer development and artist management, as well as providing world-class recording studios within the building. The striking architecture, marble accents, and unique design make this one of the most recognizable buildings on Music Row, fitting for one of the true queens of country music.

THE HEART WON'T LIE

WHAT Heart of Music Row

WHERE 40 Music Square W.

COST Free

PRO TIP It's on the south side.

And it's all surrounded by this not-so-mysterious wall that holds a mysterious secret. So while the rest of the tour is futilely trying to sneak a peek inside the writer's room windows in front of Reba's old building, you can be inspecting the wall and listening closely for the beating heart of Music Row.

Top: Stone wall around Starstruck
Inset: The Heart of Music Row

The Starstruck building has a helipad on top for when Reba would fly to work.

42 HEARTBREAK HOTEL

How is Nashville responsible for Elvis's success?

Long lost in the annals of history is any remnant or marker of the studio where Elvis Presley recorded one of his first and most famous hits, "Heartbreak Hotel." After recording his initial sessions in Memphis at the famed Sun Studios and honing his live performances on the Louisiana Hayride show, Elvis signed with RCA Records and went mainstream, starting with a trip to Nashville to record at RCA's first permanent studio in town, RCA Victor on McGavock. Armed with players like Chet Atkins on guitar, Floyd Cramer on piano, and members of the Jordanaires and Speer Family Gospel group on background vocal duty, as well as his usual trio of Scotty Moore, Bill Black, and D. J. Fontana (actually his first recording session with this band), Presley recorded the song on January 10, 1956, along with a few others over a two-day session. The success of that record put not only Elvis on the worldwide map but also elevated Nashville. After it became a massive hit, publishers, labels, songwriters, and musicians all flocked to the area to become part of the rising scene.

Elvis returned to RCA Victor to record "I Want You, I Need You, I Love You" a year later before a long and storied career at the new RCA Studio B facilities on 17th Avenue. The building was eventually demolished in 2006 to make way for a snazzy car dealership's overflow parking lot. There is unfortunately no marker to commemorate the history made on this site.

Decades later, in the 1980s, the *Crook & Chase* show was filmed in the same facility.

Top: RCA Victor building, circa 2003. Photo
courtesy of James V. Roy
Inset: The site, circa 2018

TO THE VICTOR GO THE SPOILS

WHAT The Heartbreak Hotel
studio

WHERE 1525 McGavock St.

COST Free

PRO TIP The adjacent
Demonbreun Hill strip is full
of restaurants and shops for a
refresher.

43 HERMITAGE BATHROOM

Who would take a picture of a hotel restroom?

Fact: the most photographed bathroom in America is right in downtown Nashville at the Hermitage Hotel. The men's room in the basement level of this hotel is a striking art deco tiled, black-and-lime-green-striped throne room with the perfect accents to tie it all together, restored to the same opulence it showcased in the 1930s.

Aside from being voted "Restroom of the Year" on multiple occasions, the Hermitage bathroom is also part of the whole Hermitage Hotel sophistication, so make sure you take a look around the hotel itself. The ballroom has been featured in numerous movies, whereas the Capitol Grille downstairs was where Dinah Shore was discovered singing with the Francis Craig Orchestra. A famous bellhop was . . . ah, I'm getting off track. Yes, back to the bathroom! It's been featured as the backdrop for Jack White, REM, and Alan Jackson photo sessions. The shoe-shine station is rumored to have had clientele like Elvis and JFK, and it's easily recognizable as the setting on a vast number of music videos. This is definitely a must-see if you're downtown and looking for somewhere to kill twenty minutes—and ladies, have no fear: the sign outside the door clears the way for females to pop inside the room and take a gander at the lime-colored urinals and shoe-shine stations without any consequences.

GREEN WITH ENVY

WHAT Hermitage Hotel Men's Room

WHERE 231 6th Ave N.

COST Free

PRO TIP The Capitol Grille has had numerous menu items featured on Food Network and Travel Channel shows—grab a bite.

Top: Interior of the Hermitage Hotel men's room
Inset: The Hermitage Hotel

The Hermitage Hotel has been featured in the shows *Nashville* and *Hannah Montana*, and was the residence for the billiards legend Minnesota Fats.

CHATEAU ON THE ROW (page 40)

STIX (page 172)

OPRYLAND ARCHITECTURE AND SECRETS: MAGNOLIA (page 140)

CURSE OF THE GRAND OLE OPRY (page 52)

#WhatLiftsYou
#NashvilleGulch
@KelseyMontagueArt

WEENIE'S: WHERE THE LOCALS GO (page 192)

BICENTENNIAL PARK—PART 2 (page 16)

DEMONBREUN'S CAVE (page 54)

UGLIEST STATUE IN EXISTENCE (page 188)

WILLIE NELSON, FORTUNE TELLER (page 194)

MCNAIRY SPRING (page 120)

DEMONBREUN'S GRAVE (page 56)

MOUNT OLIVET CEMETERY (page 126)

44 HOLE IN THE FLOOR

What's down there?

Just around the corner from Music Row is a local hangout called the Red Door Saloon that's got a particularly fun secret hidden in its floorboards. Inside the joint, all is right in the bar world, and to most casual observers, nothing is amiss. But hang around long enough and you'll see it happen—voices near the bar will be raised, conversations will turn to "I'm not gonna do it, YOU do it!" and "What'd you see?!" And then a brave, just-drunk-enough lagermeister will have a buddy hold his beer while he kneels down on all fours and presses his face against the floorboards, his eyeball seeking the small sliver of light projecting from this veiled enigma: a hole in the floor. He will stare for a few moments, a big smile will project across his face, and he'll get back on his feet, now enlightened, with the only appropriate response to the inquiry being "You gotta see it for yourself!"

And this is the truth: you must see it for yourself. There is no believable explanation for the spectacle that is below the floor at the Red Door, so head on in, down a few sips of liquid courage, hit those knees, and see what's underneath the surface.

An original Midtown hang, Red Door guards the current strip of local spots on Division Street.

RED DOOR DISTRICT

WHAT Mystery hole in the floor

WHERE 1816 Division Street

COST Free to enter; menu prices apply

PRO TIP Make sure you go to the right location—the East Nashville location does NOT have the hole.

Left: A curious patron has to take a peek
Right: The Red Door walkway

45 JIMI HENDRIX MURAL

Where did Jimi Hendrix get upstaged in Nashville?

In 1962, an aspiring guitarist by the name of "Jimmie" Hendrix was playing Nashville bars while serving in the Army and stationed just north of town in Ft. Campbell. Most of the popular clubs were on Jefferson Street, the hub of live music at the time, places like Club Baron, Del Morocco, and the Black Diamond, and featured the legendary likes of Duke Ellington, Ray Charles, and Little Richard. Jimmie was in a house band at the Del Morocco and making a name for himself all over town but also learning from the greats who graced the same stages.

Legend has it that one night at Club Baron, after admiring local icon Johnny Jones, Jimmie was told by Jones that he'd never be the player that Jones was. So Jimmie did what any proud ax-player would do and challenged Jones to a guitar duel. In what must have been one of the most electrifying nights in Nashville history—amps turned up, crowd screaming, guitars screaming even louder—Hendrix didn't fare too well and apparently lost the battle. But oh, what a glorious battle it must've been!

Across the street is an impressive R&B tribute mural on the east side of Eyecatchers, featuring Stevie Wonder and Marvin Gaye.

Top: The battle between Hendrix and Jones begins
Inset: Elks Lodge

BATTLE OF NASHVILLE BLUES GREATS

WHAT Elks Lodge mural

WHERE 2614 Jefferson St.

COST Free

PRO TIP Grab some Mary's Bar-B-Que right on down the road at 1106 Jefferson.

While Hendrix eventually left Nashville and changed his first name to "Jimi," this particular night in his year-long residency is commemorated by a huge mural on the side of the Club Baron, now the Elks Lodge on Jefferson.

46 LABYRINTH

Where can I find personal enlightenment the Nashville way?

Lucky for you, there's just the place in Nashville. With a number of outdoor labyrinths peppering the city, the most accessible is a seven-circuit medieval one on the Vanderbilt University campus near the Scarritt Bennett Center. Walkers are encouraged to experience purgation, illumination, and union, according to the guide posted at the center itself. The good news is that walking the labyrinth will help provide a meditative environment to cleanse your thoughts and your soul of the distractions of the day—and the great news is that there are no walls, so you can get out any time you want. This particular maze is open during daylight hours and is accessible through the Gilson Hall arched window that enters the International Peace Garden.

A handful of other local labyrinths are also scattered around town, primarily at churches like the Glendale United Methodist Church at 900 Glendale Lane, St. Ann's Episcopal Church at 419 Woodland Street, and Woodmont Christian Church at 3601 Hillsboro Road, as they offer their own spiritual and intellectual renewal. There are a number of other options but a lot of them are on private property, so make sure you consult an online labyrinth locator to help you find these other locations as well as yourself in your journey.

Scarritt Bennett Center Mission: "to create space where individuals and groups engage each other to achieve a more just world."

Scarritt Bennett Labyrinth

PEACE OF MIND

WHAT Scarritt Bennett Labyrinth

WHERE 1000 19th Ave S.

COST Free

PRO TIP The small parking lot on Grand Ave, just east of 19th Ave, is the perfect access point.

47 LOCK ONE PARK

Why do those stairs go down to the river?

Most Nashvillians have never visited the Lock One Park and most probably don't even know it exists. As one of the city's smallest parks, it might be one of the most fascinating, with a standing history of walls and remnants that can still be seen within the grounds. To the well-travelled observer, it might be more reminiscent of a Mayan ruin or similar to the tiers of Machu Picchu, and to the frequent visitor, Lock One Park has a spiritual energy and an isolation that can't be felt in any other park.

Ensconced at the park are the stone remains of a twentieth-century feat of engineering that was intended to control the flow of the adjacent Cumberland River. In the early 1900s, the U.S. Army Corps of Engineers built a series of twenty-one dams and locks between Nashville and Smith's Shoals, Kentucky, in order to provide smoother waterways for rivercraft, like steamboats and barges. Unfortunately, the dams and locks didn't have the intended effect on the river, and the structures were either destroyed by dynamite or left to submerge. Lock One Park contains the shoreline and cliffside remains of the first lock, which was actually built on the previous site of Heaton's Station, one of Nashville's original pioneer forts from the 1700s. While the fort disappeared long ago, the lock was not demolished until October 1954, and the ruins are now maintained by Metro Parks.

LOCKED UP

WHAT Lock One Park

WHERE Lock Road

COST Free

PRO TIP This is a good place to throw a line in the water.

Top: The stairs leading down to the lock
Above left: Riverfront ruins
Above right: Remnants in the woods

Further down, a crumbling sidewalk precariously hovers above the river—a great visual but not a good place for a stroll.

48 LOVE CIRCLE

Where is there a Lover's Lane around this town?

Just off West End and I-440, up a road that looks like you don't have any earthly business traveling on, lies a secret little jewel of Nashville: Love Circle. The winding road leading up to this hilltop crest can be harrowing and misleading, but resist gravity and keep the wheels rolling up, clamber the hill after you get the car parked, and you'll be rewarded with a spectacular sight of downtown. Be warned, though—the view that unfolds will be inspiring. If you're a neighborhood teen, you're going to be hanging out here a lot through those high school years, grabbing selfies up on top of the circle. If you're 45 and want to bust out a blanket on the grass, you'll feel like a teen again. And if you're there on a 4th of July evening with the fireworks exploding over downtown . . . well, you're about to have an awesome night.

The most unfortunate aspect of this old Civil War earthwork and reservoir known as Love Circle is the presence of Mount Richmore, country star John Rich's cube-like residence that blocks out a fair share of the skyline. But as for the rest of the circle, it's a quiet little loop of street overlooking the city that, on the right night, you just might have all to yourself.

LOVE IS A WONDERFUL THING

WHAT Love Circle Viewpoint

WHERE Love Circle

COST Free

PRO TIP Bring your camera!

Top: Nashville skyline
Above left: Mt. Richmore
Above right: The hills of Civil War earthworks

This part of the hillside is a Civil War earthwork with clear evidence showing in the characteristic mounds and notches.

49 LUAU ISLAND

Wanna get away?

Imagine a world that is literally fifteen minutes away from the hustle and bustle of the downtown metropolitan area but is as remote and isolated as a Polynesian island. Good news for your imagination: there actually is such an island—one of many, in fact—that is peeking out of the water of the Percy Priest Lake a few miles east of downtown off I-40. Percy Priest is a man-made lake that submerged the area when an Army Corps of Engineers dam went up and flooded 14,000 acres in 1968. Luau Island is one of the smaller and more personal options in the outcropping of island peaks, covered only in sand and a few trees and providing a perfect setting for a few hours or even an overnight getaway. Camping is allowed but you might have to share the island with other visitors. While still generally a Nashville secret, it's well known to the boaters and kayakers in the area, and those are pretty much the only ways to get to Luau—by boat, kayak, paddleboard, etc.

PARADISE FOUND

WHAT Luau Island

WHERE Percy Priest Lake via Elm Hill Marina—3361 Bell Road

COST Island is free but Elm Hill Marina is $8 to use boat launch.

PRO TIP Go early to stake your claim.

Remnants of Old Hickory Boulevard are still visible on many islands of the lake, though most of it was covered over when the area was flooded.

Top: Approaching Luau Island
Above: On the island

You can also choose from a number of other islands of all shapes, sizes, and topographies, based on your preference, but if you plan to stay overnight, do a little research to make sure camping is allowed and find out if any fire permits are needed.

50 MARTHA'S QUARRY

What happens when a quarry digs too deep?

Once upon a time, there was a rock quarry in Wilson County that had been going full steam ahead for over forty years when, one day, it hit a fissure and began to fill up with water. There was no time to get all the equipment removed and the site has been frozen in time beneath the surface, ever since. Until recently, for scuba divers there was plenty to look at and explore in the 58 feet of water: four quarry buildings, a rock crusher, and the adjacent houses are still standing, and a transport bus, at least thirty sunken boats—one of which is apparently a sailboat marooned in a trench—litter the floor of the lake. Divers also reported seeing bluegill, bass, koi, and catfish.

Back in the day, up to eighty divers a weekend would visit Martha's Quarry, paying $20 a day for tickets sold through local dive shops, but lo and behold, developers have since bought the property from the previous owner and the site is now off limits to the public. Sorry to get your hopes up. If you need a dive option for your fix, you might need to drive an hour or two to get to the next best option, said to be Loch Low-Minn, another quarry lake, near Athens.

UNDER THE SURFACE

WHAT Abandoned underwater quarry

WHERE 584 Quarry Rd.

COST N/A

PRO TIP Find a legal option for your diving needs.

Submerged structures and items can be seen from a Google Maps view of the lake.

Top: Martha's Quarry. Photo courtesy of Lisa Erickson.
Above: Under the surface. Photo courtesy of Easy Divers.

51 MCNAIRY SPRING

Why is Nashville here?

Back in those roaring 1700s, when America was expanding westward and pioneers were claiming land faster than they could buy it, French fur trader Timothy Demonbreun was exploring the region by river, and he noticed some muddy drainage coming out of a creek into the Cumberland just north of current downtown Nashville. Being the wise explorer that he was, he strongly suspected that one thing in particular was causing the water to muddy: lots and lots of wildlife. To his pleasant unsurprise, he was right—up the riverbank was a plethora of turkey, bison, and other creatures all attracted to this area by one particular feature: the natural sulphur springs. McNairy Spring in Bicentennial Park is one such spring and can still be seen flowing on the original spot.

As you may know from other features in this book, Demonbreun settled in the area, and Nashville is an "It" city of the United States, all thanks to this spring. The water still flows the same path to the river, although it has long since been converted to a drainage tunnel rather than a babbling brook. Get the perfect selfie in front of the McNairy Spring and bring home some true Nashville history.

A bike path now follows the creek past the baseball stadium to the Cumberland River.

The site of the original spring

SPRING INTO NASHVILLE

WHAT Sulphur Springs

WHERE 998 7th Ave N.

COST Free

PRO TIP Park at the Farmers' Market and make that part of your trip.

52 MERIWETHER LEWIS'S GRAVE

You mean the guy from Lewis and Clark?

One of the original pioneers of westward expansion, Meriwether Lewis of the Lewis and Clark Expedition, hung his final hat in the hills of Tennessee, taking to the grave the secret of his untimely death.

As we learned in school, Mr. Lewis, along with William Clark, was appointed by President Jefferson to find a direct route to the Pacific. This two-year, eight-thousand-mile journey was well-chronicled, and their path to the Oregon coast made them legends of their time and two of the most famous men in America. However, after the journey, Meriwether didn't fare so well with the fame and his sense of purpose, despite his salary, land-grant, and appointment as governor of the Louisiana Territory.

In October 1809, Lewis was travelling to Washington, D.C. via the Natchez Trace, an old Indian trail that connected Natchez, Mississippi, to Nashville, when he stopped for the

GRINDER'S STAND ON THE NATCHEZ TRACE

WHAT Meriwether Lewis Grave

WHERE Milepost 385.9 on the Natchez Trace Parkway

COST Free

PRO TIP Take the whole day for a leisurely drive along this world-famous scenic route.

On your journey, you might cross the Parkway Bridge, a 155-foot-high, award-winning, double-arched spectacle covering 1,648 feet of he valley.

Top left: Meriwether Lewis's grave
Top right: Parkway Bridge
Above right: This way to the Old Trace

evening at Grinder's Stand, a trading post on the Trace near Hohenwald, Tennessee. Here's where things get murky: differing eyewitness accounts claim that Lewis either a) got really liquored up and committed suicide, or b) was murdered by unknown assailant. There is strong weight to either argument. Given Lewis's mental state at the time, suicide was a possibility. However, based on the account from Mrs. Grinder, three men arrived and challenged Lewis to a duel outside, which supports the murder theory.

The grave, about seventy miles southwest of Nashville, is marked by a broken column at milepost 385.9 on the Natchez Trace Parkway, one of the most cherished drives in the state.

53 MOUSE HOUSE

Where's the legendary Mouse House?

When visiting the Nashville Public Library, keep your eye out for a shadowy ball of fur skirting the edges of the walls, roaming the halls, and making you wonder if your eyes are deceiving you. *Wait, what's that . . . could that be . . . a mouse?!* If that's a conversation you're having with yourself, you've just experienced a rare sighting of Buttercup, a mouse who has made the library her home, quite literally, since the 1960s. Don't believe it? Well, just look down toward those floorboards in the children's section of the library and you'll see her house! Back in the '50s, when the library was in its previous location downtown, Buttercup's original abode was built by Tom Tichenor, a library volunteer and later staff member who constructed Buttercup's single-story, red brick home with a yellow roof and a chimney. She moved locations along with the library, first to the Ben West Library in 1963 and then, most recently, to the current location on Church Street. Along the way, Buttercup must've done well for herself, as she has moved from the modest brick home still standing at the base of the front pillar and now lives in a three-story columned mansion, towering twelve inches high and displaying her name clearly across the facade.

RODENTERTAINER

WHAT Buttercup's houses

WHERE 615 Church St.

COST Free

PRO TIP Get your parking validated at the checkout counter.

Top left: Buttercup's humble beginnings
Top right: Buttercup's new mansion
Above left: The library's marionette collection

If you get down on the floor and peer in her door, Buttercup might not be home, but thousands of kids have seen her lounging by a fireplace or at home in a castle or even in her bedroom with furniture. You can also write a letter to Buttercup to leave in the nearby mail slot where she'll be sure to read it upon her return home.

While at the library, be sure to visit the marionette collection, also by Tom Tichenor, and a famed assortment in itself.

Where is the coolest cemetery in town?

Not that cemeteries are a fun place to go to, but if you're into that sort of thing, Mount Olivet has some of the most unique and historical tombs and gravestones in town. Established in 1856 and named after Jerusalem's Mount of Olives, from which Jesus Christ is presumed to have ascended to heaven, it houses a number of former Tennessee governors and statesmen, as well as many other prominent figures from the state's history. A stroll through the grounds will reveal intriguing architecture and mysterious areas, each with its own fascinating story.

The first area of note is the Confederate Circle in the center of the grounds defined by a circular 26,588-square-foot grassy area with a frequently vandalized obelisk at its center. An estimated 1,500 Confederate soldiers are said to be buried within the circle.

Another photo-worthy monument is that of Vernon K. Stevenson, a war-profiteering railroad president who is buried in an exact replica of Napoleon Bonaparte's tomb as a tribute to one of Napoleon's descendants who invested in Stevenson's career.

And what gothic cemetery would be complete without a pyramid? There are some intricate details to this one, though—Mt. Olivet's pyramid is a duplicate of the Great Pyramid of Cheops in Giza, Egypt, complete with sphinxes and identical celestial orientation (note the bronze arrows in the walkway marking this alignment). The structure itself inters

Cornelia Fort, the first female pilot to be killed in the line of military duty, is buried at Mt. Olivet as well.

Confederate Circle

BURIED HISTORY

WHAT Mt. Olivet Cemetery

WHERE 1101 Lebanon Pike

COST Free

PRO TIP Maps and guides are available in the main office.

the remains of Major E.C. Lewis, an industrialist in the late 1800s who ran the Centennial Exposition in 1897. Aside from the full-scale replica of the Greek Parthenon, the other main attraction at the fair was a replica of an Egyptian pyramid. And what's more fitting for Mr. Lewis's eternal rest than a model tribute to his achievement with the Exposition?

Let's not forget other notables whose resting places lay within the property: Nashville legend Thomas Ryman; plantation owner Adelicia Acklen; politician John Bell; women's suffrage activist Anne Dallas Dudley; HCA founders Thomas Frist and Jack C. Massey; singer Vern Gosdin; entrepreneur E. Bronson Ingram; Confederate general William Jackson; founder of Lipscomb University, David Lipscomb; Mayor Randal William McGavock; historical icon John Overton; music industry legend Fred Rose; and the innocent and tragic Marcia Trimble, among thousands of others.

Ah, and the ghosts! Mt. Olivet is known for being a hotbed of paranormal activity in Nashville. Wandering apparitions are frequently seen, spiritual drifters called "black abbeys" are often spotted wandering between mausoleums, and even Thomas Ryman himself has been rumored to have been seen stumbling amongst the headstones.

⁵⁵ MURALS

Why is Nashville art larger than life?

Nashville is pretty hip, in case you haven't heard. One of the reasons is the exploding art scene, not only because of the cool bike racks, random guitars, turkeys, and catfish around town, but also due to the murals plastered everywhere. The theme of each of the murals is different but the motivations behind them are the same: expressionism . . . commissions . . . advertisements . . . graffiti . . . historical tributes . . . and randomness.

So where exactly should you be looking for them? Here is a list of the mural displays—both the prominent and the secret—all over town.

- 12 South
  I Believe in Nashville—2702 12th Ave. S.
  Nashville at Heart—2705 12th Ave. S.

- The Gulch
  The Wings—230 11th Ave. S.

- The Nations
  Lee Estes Portrait—1407 51st Ave. N.

- Jefferson Street
  Jimi Hendrix and Johnny Jones—2614 Jefferson St.
  Blues Tribute—Jefferson St. between 26th and 27th Ave.
  Gateway to Heritage—Jefferson St. underneath I-40 overpass

- Downtown
  Wall of Cash—300 4th Ave. S.
  I Believe in Nashville 2—1402 Clinton St.
  Legends Corner—428 Broadway
  12th & Porter—114 12th Ave. N.
  Off the Wall—3020-3098 Charlotte Ave.

Nashville At Heart

THE MURAL OF THE STORY

WHAT Nashville street art

WHERE Everywhere!

COST Free

PRO TIP Look for forced perspectives as well as interactive murals.

- Music Row
  Dueling Cowboys—24 Music Square W.
  Hillsboro Village Dragon—2102 Belcourt Ave.
- House of Blues
  The entire studio campus at 518 E. Iris Dr.

Arguably the most secret and fascinating mural in town is the realism of artist Brian Tull featured in the Uptown Underground parking garage underneath 2034 West End Ave. These hidden gems corner the creepy dark garage market with unbelievable paintings highlighting automobiles and chrome reflections that most viewers swear are photographs. Make sure to see these three on display in this subterranean gem, *The Highway Has Always Been Your Lover*, Anabell, and *Before We Abandoned It Out West*.

Bear in mind that this list just scratches the surface of the literally hundreds of murals throughout town. Just keep your eyes peeled, because any street corner is within a stone's throw of a painted creation, and more are revealed every day.

The fifteen-story silo mural in the Nations is of neighborhood resident Lee Estes, painted by renowned artist Guido Van Helten.

MURDER ON MUSIC ROW

Who killed Kevin Hughes?

Sometimes Nashville's secrets can't be kept, no matter how hard she tries to keep them. Sometimes she leaves little clues that take years, if not decades, to piece together, as in the unusual fate of Kevin Hughes. In 1989, Kevin was a chart researcher for *Cash Box* magazine, a respected music trade paper that ranked new and established artists and their singles. For Kevin, the job was a dream come true, working in the burgeoning country music industry and under the watchful eye of industry veteran Richard "Tony" D'Antonio, *Cash Box*'s director of Nashville operations. As he became more comfortable and experienced in his position, Kevin began to see small discrepancies in the accounting and realized that *Cash Box* was doing the unthinkable: taking "payola," a form of illegal incentive whereby an artist/label influences a chart position by bribes of money or things of value.

TRAGEDY ON MUSIC ROW

WHAT The Cash Box Murder

WHERE 1020 16th Ave. S.

COST Free

PRO TIP Mamas, don't let your babies grow up to be in the music business.

According to reports, Kevin Hughes was about to blow the whistle on the payola operation by going public with the presumed scandal when he and his buddy, Sammy Sadler, were randomly attacked by a masked gunman outside of Sammy's record label, Evergreen Records, on March 9. Kevin ran south on 16th Ave but was shot twice and died at the scene. Sadler was shot as well but survived. Because Kevin and Sammy were at Evergreen unexpectedly, the police assumed that the encounter was a completely random one and that the men were simply in the wrong place at the wrong time.

Left: Evergreen Records original log cabin
Right: The site of the tragic ambush

Time passed without any leads or breaks in the case—Kevin and Sammy's story was featured on *Unsolved Mysteries*, *Cold Case Files*, and *Fatal Encounters*, and Nashville was content to keep the identity of the murderer its mistress. That is, until investigators finally pieced together clues like bullet forensics, witness testimonials, and cat hair evidence that linked a suspect to the scene . . . and Tony D'Antonio himself was arrested in 2002. It was determined that D'Antonio and his *Cash Box* associate, Chuck Dixon, had conspired to commit the murder to keep Kevin quiet and that D'Antonio had ultimately pulled the trigger in the ambush.

Tony D'Antonio was convicted and sentenced to life in prison, where he died in September 2014. What has become known as the Music Row murders serves as a reminder that when you get down to the nitty gritty, music is still a ruthless business, and money is the root of all evil.

Issues of *Cash Box* magazine can be found in antique stores around town, such as Antique Archaeology, made famous by the TV show *American Pickers*.

Why are there giant naked people dancing on Music Row?

If you watch any travel show that spotlights Nashville, you are guaranteed to see two local landmarks: the popular Parthenon and the circle of giant naked statues at the heart of Music Row known as *Musica*. This sculpture was commissioned in 2003 as an urban renewal project and is the brainchild of Alan LeQuire, a local artist who has designed and sculpted other projects around town, such as the Athena statue inside the Parthenon and the Women's Suffrage Memorial. As you can imagine, being in the buckle of the Bible Belt, there were plenty of shocked faces on the locals when *Musica* was revealed to contain a whole lot of oversized nakedness staring them right in the eye.

The statue was requested to represent music as a whole, and it was difficult for many to see how this particular statue could reflect music at all other than the hoisted tambourine. This is where the secret comes in, and it is a very ingenious one in Mr. LeQuire's explanation. You see, if you look closely, you will notice that the figures are bursting from the ground in an explosive manner, thus representing the moment that an idea is created. Plus, the figures are obviously naked,

Musica sits on the site of Fort Houston, one of Nashville's first forts. It is also just down the road from the original flagship Tin Roof bar, where stars like Lee Brice, Chris Young, Jarrod Niemann, and many others have been found throwing a few back.

Left: An original Musica model
Right: Musica

expressing the rawness of the fresh idea. The tambourine itself is a fairly universal instrument used in multiple cultures and all genres so as not to be too specific. And everyone in the circle is dancing, which is the only way to truly convey music in sculpture. So, while the untrained eye might just see some random naked statues (and refer to them with that description in casual conversation) that occasionally get dressed up in oversized costumes per the upcoming holiday, there is much more depth to these forms once you're in the know.

133

Where can I see behind the curtain of the music industry?

Tucked away underneath the once-prominent Municipal Auditorium is the most unsuspecting museum and one of the best kept secrets in town—the Musicians Hall of Fame. Yes, the Country Music Hall of Fame a few blocks away gets all the glory and is a must-see while in town, but the Musicians HOF covers even wider industry ground and offers some of the more unique items on display from all of music, not just country, from the players who made the songs you know by heart sound so good. Kind of like a hardcore Hard Rock Café wall, this place specializes in the instruments and equipment that recorded classic songs across all genres. It's where you can see the original soundboard from Jack's Track studios, where Garth Brooks recorded all of his records, as well as Crystal Gayle's "Don't It Make My Brown Eyes Blue" and Kathy Mattea's "18 Wheels and a Dozen Roses"; where you can see the stage where Jimi Hendrix played on Jefferson Street, find the original lathe that cut Elvis's first record, rock the bass played on Springsteen's "Born To Run," experience the vocal booth that Elvis recorded in,

UNSUNG HEROES

WHAT Musicians Hall of Fame

WHERE 401 Gay Street

COST $24.00

PRO TIP Put this attraction near the top of your Nashville "To-Do" list.

On-site is a one-of-a-kind interactive Grammy Museum Gallery for visitors to explore the history of the Grammy Awards.

Top left: An historic Fender Stratocaster on display
Top right: Municipal Auditorium
Above right: Sun's services

and see instruments used by the Beach Boys, Simon & Garfunkel, Bob Dylan, Bob Seger, the Mamas & the Papas, the Jackson 5, Stevie Wonder, and even the Beatles, all just quick examples of the hundreds of artifacts and exhibits. The most famous names in studio recording are also represented, from the Swampers, the Funk Brothers, the Wrecking Crew, and the A-Team, all the way from Detroit to Muscle Shoals and LA to New York.

This is one of those Nashville secrets hiding in plain sight and easily one of the best experiences for the deeper music fan.

NUN BUN

Who stole the Nun Bun?

As Seen On TV: A Christmas miracle is said to have happened on December 25, 1996, at Bongo Java in the Belmont area of town: a cinnamon roll came out of the oven that had a striking resemblance to Mother Teresa. The coffee shop quickly put up a website and had a cult-like following, appearing on worldwide news stories, getting a segment on *The Late Show with David Letterman*, and even drawing the attention and admiration of the head nun herself. Although she would not allow her name to be attached to any sales of any related merchandise, she was all good with the moniker of "Nun Bun" and the sweet roll was put on display, becoming a popular local draw.

Flash forward to nine years later: the owners show up to the store on Christmas Day (again!) in 2005 to find the front door removed from its hinges and the display case emptied of its holy cargo. Bongo Java became world famous again but this time for more nefarious reasons. No ransom note, no explanation, no trace of the bun has ever been found, save for a sketchy rumored sighting in Seattle, but Bongo Java still has a standing $5,000 reward for the safe return of the saintly dough.

The case is still on full display in the waiting line with a "Nun Buns of Steel" replica of the bun in the original's place, and an interactive story to regale you with its tragic tale.

The Bongo Java restroom is where songwriter Karen Staley got the idea to write the Faith Hill classic "Take Me as I Am."

The Legendary NunBun™

The NunBun™ was discovered by long-time employee Ryan Finney in October 1996 and became world famous soon after - including shots on Morning Edition, Late Night with David Letterman and (as we've been told) a Calcutta newspaper.

Mother Teresa enjoyed the silliness of the bun. She also has to be called Mother Teresa Miracle Bun and Immaculate Confection and didn't want us to use her image for any advertising or fund-raising purposes - which she enjoyed as a personal letter sent through her attorney.

She joked about the NunBun™ jauntily before she died even though to a point where we could sell stamps merchandise and couldn't even produce these sweeties. She also jokingly told her attorney that she wished someone to steal a bun that looks like her someday.

The NunBun™ was stolen on Christmas Day 1995.

PRAY FOR ITS RETURN

WHAT The Nun Bun

WHERE 2007 Belmont Blvd.

COST Price of a cup of coffee

PRO TIP Explore the Belmont University campus across the street.

Top: The Nun Bun on display
Above: Replica of the Nun Bun

Where does Oprah get her hair cut?

It's no secret that Nashville is home to whole lot of celebrities but, save for Reese Witherspoon, most of them are transplants; Nashville tends to pull high-profile superstars into her orbit due to the downhome anonymous nature of the town that provides a comfortable backdrop away from the bigger city life on the West Coast. However, one meteoric celebrity made her way to Nashville, not to escape the rigors of fame or to be a singer, but to simply start a better life: Ms. Oprah Winfrey.

Oprah first made her way to Music City at twelve years old to live with her father, a barber, and to escape a more dangerous lifestyle in Milwaukee. After a bit of a rough start in Nashville, she eventually flourished, becoming active in student council and debate club at East High School (110 Gallatin Ave). She then became Ms. Black Nashville and won a full scholarship to Tennessee State University after winning an Elks Club (2614 Jefferson St.) speaking contest. She developed her own talk show on the local Nashville CBS affiliate, NewsChannel 5/WTVF (474 James Robertson Pkwy), and became the city's first African American news co-anchor while nineteen years old and still in college. She ultimately dropped out of college at TSU (but later completed her degree and graduated) to pursue her career in broadcasting, and needless to say, it's worked out well for her. Oprah became a self-made billionaire at age forty-nine and is one of the most recognizable personalities in the world.

FAMILY OWNED

WHAT Oprah's father's barber shop

WHERE Winfrey Barber and Beauty Shop, 1001 Lischey Ave.

COST Services vary

PRO TIP Walk-ins welcome

Top: Winfrey's Barber Shop
Above left: East High School
Above right: NewsChannel 5

Oprah's father, Vernon, whom she credits for her educational enthusiasm, is still in Nashville and running the same barber shop that he's had for over fifty years now. There was some conflict over the shop, but Oprah bought the building herself, and the Winfrey Barber and Beauty Shop is still open for business in East Nashville.

NewsChannel 5 was also where *Hee Haw* and *Candid Camera* were filmed.

61 OPRYLAND ARCHITECTURE AND SECRETS: MAGNOLIA

What's the big deal about the Opryland Hotel?

No trip to Nashville is complete without a visit or stay at the Opryland Resort and Convention Center, the largest non-gambling resort east of the Mississippi. Days can be spent wandering the halls and seeing the obvious wonders, like the riverboat ride, the shooting water fountains, and the art displays. But it's what's not so obvious to the eye that is worth looking out for in this iconic building.

Starting in the Magnolia lobby, which was the entrance to the original Opryland Hotel back in 1977 that lodged visitors to the nearby Opryland USA theme park, the first thing that will grab the attention will be the grand staircase. Make no mistake, this was indeed fashioned after the Tara staircase from *Gone with the Wind* and may also bring to mind a few scenes from *Titanic*. The Tiffany-style chandelier hanging above it is the original and is lowered once a month for cleaning. But keep your eye out for The Lady in Black, the ghost of Mrs. McGavock, whose family owns the land that the hotel sits on. She's mostly seen at night, observing from the shadows but has been spotted descending the staircase for what is surely a terrifying moment for the housekeepers.

Adjacent to the staircase is the shop Cowboys and Angels, where you can find a Swarovski crystal-encrusted mirror with a price tag of $12,000, if you're in the market.

650 WSM Studio

SWEET MAGNOLIA

WHAT Opryland Hotel Magnolia Wing

WHERE 2800 Opryland Dr

COST Free

PRO TIP Watch for the carpet changing color—than means you're entering a new wing.

At this point, if you go straight behind the staircase, working your way down the line of restaurants, you'll eventually reach a wall of murals where a few secrets are waiting. The creation of this mural is a trivia topic: it took fifteen months in 1976 for T. Max Hostettler and his Austin Peay State University students to paint the panels of this 2,200-square-foot mural in a high school gym, hanging them from the walls like wallpaper. The scenes depict Nashville life in the 1880s and feature some well-known landmarks from the area, as well as faces of people that Hostettler knew personally. There's also some brain-spinning forced perspective happening in the street scene, as well as a hard-to-miss phallic symbol over by the staircase.

Now, back to the staircase . . . if you'd have gone right instead of straight, here's a look down that hall. Immediately on your left will be the current location of 650 WSM, the home of the Grand Ole Opry radio show. Chances are, in the morning you'll see any number of singers and big-name stars interviewing with the DJs, all of whom you can watch right through the window. There's also an in-depth history of the station on the hallway wall worth spending a few minutes at.

OPRYLAND ARCHITECTURE AND SECRETS: GARDEN & CASCADES

That's great–now where?

The next area you'll come to is the Garden Conservatory, the first addition to the original hotel in 1983, which added 467 new rooms and features a Victorian-style tropical oasis with over 10,000 plants of 212 species, thirty types of palm trees, twenty types of banana plants, and a winding pathway through waterfalls. Along your stroll, you'll see thirteen small random marble statues of children in ponds and on pedestals that were imported from Italy—there were originally fourteen, but one has mysteriously disappeared along the way due to some sticky fingers. Something to bear in mind during this portion is that the entire hotel was engulfed by five-to-ten feet of water in the flood of 2010, and this entire garden was even deeper with its sunken features. The hotel didn't reopen for six months after a $250 million renovation.

In the next section, the Cascades (the second addition to the hotel in May 1988 with 824 new rooms), you'll find a huge, wide-open atrium full of restaurants and sights along the way. Take a stop in the lobby area, where you'll first notice the prominent glass sculpture, a piece by Ludek Hroch that represents the resurgence of the hotel following the flood; hence its name, *Resurgence*. Next, step outside and check out the brick mural across the car path. This unique brick relief was created by Johnny Hagerman from Virginia, who carved these

---

The bar in the middle of the Cascades used to be a circular rotating bar, but it was destroyed during the 2010 flood.

Cascading Falls

CASCADING DOWN

WHAT Opryland Hotel Cascades Wing

WHERE 2800 Opryland Dr.

COST Free

PRO TIP Cascades is the most convenient valet and transport pickup/dropoff location.

images into unfired brick at home before sending them to Kingsport to be fired. They were then delivered to the hotel and installed one by one. The scenes are classic Nashville, with the Ryman Auditorium and Roy Acuff and Minnie Pearl hanging out in front, and Andrew Jackson with the *General Jackson* showboat set against the Nashville skyline.

Back inside the Cascades lobby, the glass dome in the ceiling has some secrets as well. Some Tennessee state icons are represented in the details, such as the state insect (the ladybug), the state flower (the purple iris), a hidden state bird (a mockingbird), and several musical instruments paying homage to Tennessee's place in music history. Stepping back into the Cascades atrium, take a few moments to watch the Dancing Waters, a pond with water that jumps as patrons pass by and trigger the motion sensors. And those fish in there are Japanese goldfish, in case you're wondering. Stroll around to the back of the nearby waterfall and feel the roar of the water from behind the falls, a picture-worthy favorite of most visitors. And straight up above the escalators with the bay windows is the Porter Wagoner Presidential Suite. For a mere $3,600 per night (as of last check), you can see this suite that was named for the music legend himself that features an "all Porter, all the time" vibe with photos of Porter, some of his outlandish outfits, and a neon jukebox.

63 OPRYLAND ARCHITECTURE AND SECRETS: DELTA

How big IS this place?!

And finally, to the Delta portico, the third and final additional so far, with 922 rooms added in 1996. At the time, this addition was the largest construction project in Nashville history, with a 4.5-acre atrium, a quarter-mile river, and a New Orleans theme threaded through the décor. The rust and dirt all over the buildings are actually painted on in order to give that authentic bayou look. More plants pepper the Delta, but keep your eye out for the rare Coccoloba plant, an extremely rare find in any setting, let alone a hotel. The main feature of the Delta is the Delta River, full of catfish and coins as well as people in a riverboat cruise enjoying the meander through the waters. The waters themselves contain 1,700 samples from waterways all over the world, all sent in from locals of those areas and listed on the thirten plaques along the river walkway. However, the flood diluted the initial blend, so work is constantly under way to mix things up again.

Other finds in the Delta are the 3,000-pound wrought iron chandelier, which takes five housekeepers eight hours to clean, and a fountain nearby that becomes the stand for the forty-nine-foot Christmas tree during the holidays. There's also the Delta Fountain show, with 106 jets and an eightyl-five-foot geyser, all choreographed to music during the nightly displays. Point your eyes upward to see the two-story Dolly Parton

---

In the Delta alone, there are 6,200 half-inch-thick pieces of glass that make up the skylight ceiling, with each pane weighing 250 pounds apiece and installed by helicopter.

The Delta Atrium

Presidential Suite, where Dolly herself has stayed, as well as Oprah, Rush Limbaugh, and Presidents Ford, Reagan, Bush Jr, and Clinton.

And finally, one of the biggest draws to the hotel (one million visitors in November and December alone) are the Christmas lights, something everyone should strive to see in their lifetime. The interior of the hotel is decorated with extreme detail: fifteen miles of garland, 15,000 poinsettias, ten miles of ribbon, and the aforementioned forty-nine-foot tree, for starters. However, the exterior is where the magic happens: every branch of every tree in the main drive gets decorated with one of 20,000 strands to total over 2,000,000 LED lights. The decorating begins in July, with a full four-month lead up to the display.

And now you know a few of the secrets of the Opryland Hotel.

DELTA DAWN

WHAT Opryland Hotel Delta Wing

WHERE 2800 Opryland Dr.

COST Free

PRO TIP Take the free Opryland Hotel tour with your very own guide—info at the front desk.

PARTHENON VASE

Do you see it?

The full-scale replica of the Parthenon will definitely be a stop along any tour of Nashville—it's one of the most photographed and television-featured icons within the city. And the wonders inside are definitely worth investigating, as well. But it's one of the architectural wonders that is hidden in plain sight on the outside that makes for a secret feature.

One might think I'm talking about the red and blue color in the frieze design . . . but nope! While that color scheme is interesting and historically accurate, that's not quite the secret. No, instead, look down the interior side of the long colonnade of Doric columns that surround the structure. Now look between the columns, at the void of space that separates them. Notice anything in particular? Like one of those weird 3D posters where the image suddenly pops out at you and you can't un-see it, the same should happen here: instantaneously, you will see the shape of an Egyptian-style vase in the gap. While many count this simply as a random byproduct of the optical refinements of the columns, others maintain its intentionality as evidence of the amphora-influenced Greek architecture. Either way, it is something to see and a good conversation starter for fellow park-goers.

THE VASE IN THE SPACE

WHAT Parthenon vase

WHERE 2500 West End Ave.

COST Free

PRO TIP Plan your visit during a festival or concert taking place on the grounds.

Top: Nashville's full-scale replica of the Parthenon
Inset: The vase space

Due south down the fairway of the park is a Marriott Hotel—this is the hotel where ESPN news reporter Erin Andrews was not-so-secretly videotaped through her peephole.

65 PATTERSON HOUSE

How hard is it to speakeasy?

(The following should be read with a New York, mafia-type accent):

Psst . . . hey. Yeah, you! You want to know one of the worst kept secrets in town? It's called the Patterson House, right in the heart of Music Row . . . and with homemade bitters and spherical ice balls made one at a time, it's Nashville's first, and perhaps finest, craft cocktail establishment.

But hey, wait, slow down—this ain't your typical beer joint. They got HOUSE RULES if you want to imbibe. For instance, once you put your name on the list, you cannot enter beyond the beads—they're there for a reason, so be patient and wait your turn, paisan. Also, there will be no cell phone use (but yes, you can go ahead and text if there's something THAT important), so you might as well turn it off and enjoy the circle you're in. No standing and hovering—you have to have a seat in order to get a drink. And men—you cannot approach the ladies unless invited, so no creeping!

This experience ain't the cheapest in town, either, and you won't find any two-for-one specials, but the dark ambiance and sophisticated vibe make it easily worth it to enjoy the unique concoctions and the company you'll be keeping.

PEACEFUL SPEAKEASY FEELING

WHAT Patterson House

WHERE 1711 Division St

COST Libations vary

PRO TIP When looking for this venue, keep your eyes peeled: a small sign on the door is all you'll find.

Patterson House's unassuming entrance

A number of the books in the establishment that the barkeeps use to bring the check have been signed by Jack White, the musician/producer/ guitarist extraordinaire and frequent regular.

66 PEACE SIGN

What's the first thing I'll see on the flight in?

A few meters southeast of the bustling Nashville International Airport is a heartwarming message carved out of the tree line and visible only to those occupying the airspace above—an unmistakably ginormous circular peace sign oriented toward the northwest, directly in the path of the primary runways. Very little is known of the origin of this peculiar and nearly four-hundred-foot-diameter carving, but it's not hard to extrapolate the message from the landowner to visitors inbound and outbound: all they are saying is give peace a chance. A number of inquisitive online forums have taken some guesses as to the genesis, as well as provided some humorous commentary, but they have also revealed that the peace sign has a more functional purpose, as pilots use the landmark as a holding position checkpoint.

The shape is on private property and is not accessible to the public: a drive-by to the area will find fences and gates, as well as an anticlimactic view from the ground level if someone was ever granted access. Your best bet is from a window seat or a peek on Google Maps. Just look near the intersection of Murfreesboro Pike and Old Murfreesboro Pike.

The nearby airport is Nashville's primary airport, with the FAA identifier of "BNA" (or Berry Field Nashville).

The peace sign from above. Photo courtesy of Google Maps.

GIVE PEACE A CHANCE

WHAT Random peace sign in the woods

WHERE 36.103400, -86.662325

COST N/A

PRO TIP Drones anyone?

67 PIANO STAIRS

Where can I play some piano with my feet?

Tucked right downtown under the neon moon of Broadway is a truly hidden Nashville secret that most locals don't even know about (mainly because they tend to avoid downtown): the massive piano keys leading up the stairs at Jimmy Buffett's Margaritaville. Not too hard to find: you got fins to the left and fins to your right, but note the stairs to your right just inside the front door. Also note how one stair is white . . . and then the next is black . . . and then they continue to alternate their pattern in a familiar piano key design for a good couple of octaves heading northward. Guess what—they actually play!! So now, before you dive into your Cheeseburger in Paradise, it's time to begin your climb. Can you do "Chopsticks"? "Pirate Looks at 40"? Beethoven's 5th (which has a whole other meaning in a Nashville bar)? Just remember that if you do try to recreate the FAO Schwartz piano dance scene from *Big*, that these are STAIRS and that you can easily fall if your ragtime gets too crazy. But if you do it right, come Monday, you will have enjoyed this rarity and maybe even gotten a start on a new melody that you can pitch to Jimmy the next time you see him.

The original Margaritaville is in Key West, the site of the massive songwriter festival that takes place every May.

STAIRS OF NOTE . . .

WHAT Margaritaville staircase

WHERE 322 Broadway

COST Free . . . but menu prices apply

PRO TIP The stairs are sometimes roped off for private events, so just ask nicely.

Top: Nashville's Margaritaville
Above left: Piano stairs

68

PREDATOR TOOTH

Why is the hockey team named the Nashville Predators?

When an NHL hockey team moves to Music City, one would suspect that they would be named something more musically appropriate, much like the Triple A baseball Nashville Sounds. However, the name that stuck back in 1998 was the intimidating but seemingly random Nashville Predators, which actually isn't quite as random as one might think.

The story goes back to 1971, when excavation began for the First America Center at 4th & Union and an unexpected crevice revealed the nine-inch fang of a *Smilodon*, otherwise known as a sabre-toothed tiger. The tooth, along with over one thousand other fragments and remains, (including nearly half of the cat itself as well as even human bones), created a national stir. While these finds are not uncommon in other places, the main fascination is that this was the first fang of its kind to have been discovered in Middle Tennessee, so it was a pretty darn big deal. The tooth and a few of its fossilizing buddies were put on display at the First America Center for a number of years, reminding passersby of the story but eventually losing prominence in the folklore of Nashville.

Enter the NHL and the story is revitalized: the New Jersey Devils move to town and are renamed in a tribute to the tiger and to the secrets that are constantly being discovered beneath our feet and all around us. You can see the bones today inside the Bridgestone Arena at the Fan Information Area.

27. Bob...
28. Racco...
29. Swamp...

FANGTASTIC

WHAT The Predator Tooth

WHERE Bridgestone Arena, 501 Broadway

COST Must have event ticket to access Fan Information Area

PRO TIP If you go to Bridgestone on game night, you'd best be wearing yellow.

Top right: The Smilodon
Above left: The display case

Bridgestone is also home to *The Highway*, a SiriusXM radio show, located adjacent to the Visitor Center.

69

"PRETTY WOMAN" HOUSE

Where did Roy Orbison write "Pretty Woman"?

Why, right here in Nashville, where many a pretty woman can be seen walking down the street! An unknown factoid hidden from the knowledge bases of most locals is that most of them have frequently passed by a truly historical and monumental location in music history. Perched on a corner just off I-65 South on Wedgewood Avenue is the house where Roy Orbison was inspired to write the classic monster hit "Pretty Woman." According to the Musicians Hall of Fame, Roy confirmed this to Rodney Crowell when they were driving around. Orbison pointed out the building, saying that he was writing in the attic, looked down at the street and saw a pretty woman walk by. Hence, a legendary and influential song was born, and the intro guitar lick is now stuck in your head.

The story might not be the most scintillating but, the fact that this building, this attic, and this window are still keeping watch over the corner where countless anonymous attractive women may have made that famous stroll makes it a secret worth knowing. Currently, a computer repair shop is housed there, so if you've got a cracked screen or a busted camera on your smartphone, you'll have the perfect excuse to go in and share the same space as some powerful but little-known Nashville history.

The classic Nashville club Douglas Corner is one block away and is still a hot spot for songwriters.

The house where the song, "Pretty Woman" was written

70

PYTHON URINAL

That cage has a lid on it, right?

At the Nashville Zoo down Nolensville Pike is a unique item that may be unrivaled in any other zoo (or restroom, for that matter). For the lucky men who enter the restroom right next to the main ticket entrance and step up to the urinal, they will come face to face with a python exhibit, complete with a live snake staring at the deeds being done. The ensuing double-takes and conversation between strangers is by design—and it often takes that extra terrarium witness to corroborate to a wife that, yes, there really IS a python in the bathroom!

The python itself is a Boelen's python, a nonvenomous species also known as a "black python," that is unique to the mountains of New Guinea. The scales on its back have a slimy dark purplish/blueish/black hue, whereas the underside is typically a lighter vibe of yellow or white. Adults can grow to be up to ten feet (yes, ten feet!) in length on a tasty diet of rodents, birds, and lizards.

The ladies do not have the same luxury of a python peeper that the guys do, although there are plans for a marmoset exhibit to share the women's restroom at another location in the park.

SLICE OF PYTHON

WHAT Python tank in restroom

WHERE 3777 Nolensville Pike

COST Adults $18, Children $13 (python display is before you enter, though)

PRO TIP Get a Backstage Pass to see behind the scenes of the animal care.

Top: Python terrarium in the men's room
Above left: Nashville Zoo
Above right: Men's room resident

Restroom easy: no python escapes have been reported at the Zoo . . . yet.

71 REDWOOD

What is the connection between Al Gore, redwood lumber, and Nashville?

There is a certain indescribable vibe that can be felt when stepping through the doors of the Café at Thistle Farms. For twenty years, Thistle Farms itself has been a haven and an outlet to "heal, empower, and employ" female victims of prostitution, addiction, and trafficking. This café is a small part of their residential program that provides employment and support. So, we should all go the café, eat their food, and buy their handmade natural products for that reason alone.

However, there is another, far less heavy or noble reason to pop into the café: in the late '90s, Al Gore (yes, former Vice President Al Gore) was dismantling an old tobacco barn near Carthage, and the wood from the barn ended up being used as flooring for the new café that Thistle Farms was building. Flash-forward a few years when a patron entered the café and asked the owners if they were aware that the floor was made of redwood—very, very rare redwood—so rare that it is now illegal to use this wood for any new construction purposes.

The café has since been renovated, and new flooring has been installed since the original began to deteriorate . . . but the redwood can still be found as the frame for the large wooden booths in front of the counter, stained black in order to better fit the overall motif.

Hours are limited: open every weekday 9 a.m. to 4 p.m., closed on weekends.

Top: Redwood benches of the cafe
Above: The Cafe at Thistle Farms

BORN IN A BARN

WHAT Redwood benches

WHERE 5122 Charlotte Ave.

COST Menu item prices

PRO TIP Explore the soap and lotion shop attached to the café.

72

SANTA'S PUB

Is Santa a drinking man?

Tucked away in the Wedgewood area of town near the fairgrounds is one of Nashville's diviest bars run by a jolly man with a white beard, Denzel Irwin. Yep, you can go ahead and call him Santa if you're in his Christmas-themed pub, enjoying two-dollar (cash only) beers, karaoke 365 nights a year, and a house band every Sunday. While it's been a local secret with a cult following of college kids and neighborhood residents since April of 2011 (after a multi-decade stint as "The Caboose"), the pub is slowly becoming a destination joint for non-locals. Fans of the TV show *Impractical Jokers* will have seen Murr sporting a Santa's Pub shirt; news of low-key hangs by celebrities like Kid Rock, Ke$ha, and members of Mumford & Sons are common; *American Idol* contestant Kree Harrison is a former bartender from there; AND it was named the #1 Dive Bar in America by *Maxim* magazine. And if all that isn't reason enough to check it out, it's just a cool place: their simple house rule is "Be Nice"—there ain't no "naughty list" at this Santa's.

So what more convincing do you need? Get your sleigh out of the garage, fire up the reindeer, and fill up your stockings at Santa's Pub.

Christmas carols are a common highlight of karaoke at any time of year.

CHRISTMAS YEAR-ROUND

WHAT Santa's Pub

WHERE 2225 Bransford Ave.

COST Beers start at $2

PRO TIP This is one of the rare bars in Nashville where smoking is allowed.

Top: Santa's from the outside
Above: The world-famous karaoke stage

73

SCHERMERHORN DESIGN

How clever were the Schermerhorn architects?

A fleeting glance at the Schermerhorn Symphony Center will elicit nods of approval and a few common terms like "columns" and "ivory." But a keen observer will discern some minute details within the design of this particular building worthy of notice.

For example, the decorative star-sapphire keystones above the windows—these are not random shapes but actually the passionflower, the state wildflower of Tennessee. And the iris, the state flower (not wildflower), is paid homage throughout the building, ornamenting elevator doors, column tops, and railing decorations.

Watch for coffee beans, a tribute to the Cheek family, founders of Maxwell House Coffee, found above elevator doors, as well as covering bolt heads on exterior window panes. Next, the pilot wheels in the railings of balconies pay respect to Ingram Industries, a barge company (now publishing giant) founded by the late husband of symphony supporter Martha Ingram.

There are also musical elements in the design, with lyres found in motifs high on the building's exterior, *The Flutist* sculpture in the 4th Avenue garden (more on this momentarily), and *The Recording Angel* sculpture highlighting the corner of 4th Avenue and Demonbreun.

The limestone relief sculpture in the north side pediment tells the tragic Greek tale of Orpheus and Eurydice. While that story alone deserves its own analysis, more subtle are

SCHERMERHORN'S SECRETS

WHAT Symphony Hall Design

WHERE 1 Symphony Place

COST Free on the outside

PRO TIP See your favorite artists perform with the symphony if you can.

The face of the Schermerhorn

the alleged *Harry Potter* references within the pediment: the three-headed dog, the owl, the snake, the lion, and the rescue of the fair maiden from the bald bad guy. One might argue it merely coincidental (or reference the mythology that Ms. Rowling drew from), but it's far more fun to imagine this relief sculpture being an intentional depiction of *Harry Potter* instead.

Don't miss the memorial to Nashville first responders on the northeast corner. The symphony hall now sits on the previous home of Nashville Fire Department Engine 9, and this memorial pays tribute with bricks from the original firehouse.

Finally, pay yours respects to Mr. Kenneth Schermerhorn himself, the namesake of the hall and the conductor of the Nashville Symphony for twenty-two years. Mr. Schermerhorn never saw the concert hall open but had his ashes buried on site below *The Flutist* sculpture on the west side of the building, just inside the gates.

The seating rows inside are stored in a fascinating manner: each row is lowered and retracted into the floor it sits on.

74 SHEL SILVERSTEIN MURAL

Why are those books falling up the wall?

If this were just any other mural, it would've just been explained in the "Murals" chapter of the book, but this one is so extremely unique that it needs its own area to be fully appreciated. Located in the unlikely location of HQ Beercade, a craft brew specialty bar on 2nd Ave, the art is essentially a wall of nothing but hundreds upon hundreds of Shel Silverstein books (mostly *The Giving Tree*) opened to random pages, spilling upward and across the ceiling into a maze of pages, with a gorgeous giant female face detailed across the pages, and rainbow bubbles flying through the piece. Also keep your eye out for spoonerisms and "runny babbits" peppered across the ceiling in the river of poetry as well.

You are correct if you get the feeling that you pretty much have to see it to get a feel for the feat that artist Kate Cloud has accomplished. And given Shel's songwriting ties to Nashville, after his famous "A Boy Named Sue" became a Johnny Cash classic (among many others released by other artists), this art piece has far more relevance to the venue than one might suspect.

Even more highlights of this bar include the free arcade games, the Banksy-inspired bar graffiti, the Alice in Wonderland restrooms, and the cassette tape wall.

Classic video games are available to play for free all around the establishment.

The start of the Shel Silverstein mural

OUT OF YOUR SHEL . . .

WHAT Shel Silverstein mural

WHERE 114 2nd Ave S.

COST Menu prices

PRO TIP Beer aficionados will appreciate the wide variety of brews available at the bar.

75 SKULL'S

Who killed Skull?

At the head of the world-famous Printer's Alley in downtown Nashville is the reopened Skull's Rainbow Room, closed for decades after its original owner, David "Skull" Schulman, was tragically killed within the establishment. Originally opened in 1948, the Room stayed open for 50 years and hosted the likes of Etta James, Patsy Cline, Bob Dylan, Johnny Cash, Waylon Jennings, and Paul McCartney (yes, THAT Paul McCartney) on its stage during that run. Seriously, go to Skull's and try to even fathom seeing McCartney or Dylan playing on this small checkered stage. (For the deep McCartney fans, he was even inspired to write "Sally G" by a girl he saw perform on this very stage.)

The glory days of Skull's all changed the night that the 80-year-old Schulman was murdered in 1998 during a robbery of the club. A cigarette vendor found him on the floor of the club with his throat slit and head crushed from being hit with a bottle. The place shuttered its doors and stayed quiet for the next seventeen years. Time didn't treat it kindly—it caught fire, was flooded, and had fallen into a high state of disrepair. That is, until 2012 brought new life to the corner club, and it was renovated over three years with a grand reopening in June 2015. It still displays a few of Skull's personal objects from the original club, like his small personal TV set sitting on a shelf or a few of Skull's own flashy jackets made by Manuel, and—of course—that original checkerboard stage.

Andy Griffith was a house comedian at Skull's for a time.

PRINTER'S ALLEY ICON

WHAT Skull's Rainbow Room

WHERE 222 Printer's Alley

COST Menu prices

PRO TIP Pop into Bourbon Street Blues next door and see where Gretchen Wilson was discovered.

Top left: The top of Printer's Alley
Top right: Skull's historic stage

So, who killed Skull? That was indeed a mystery until 2001, when a couple of carny drifters, Jason Pence and James Cavaye, were charged with the crime. Pence had apparently worked for Skull for a stretch and remembered the roll of cash that he kept in his overalls. The rest was just greed and waiting for the right moment to strike with his accomplice, Cavaye. Cavaye was sentenced to life for the actual murder, whereas Pence received 15 to 25 years' imprisonment for "masterminding" the crime.

76 SNOWBALL-THROWING BEARS

What's up with the random bears having a snowball fight on the street corner?

Nashville is a hot and humid southern sweathouse in the summer months, so it definitely makes one wonder, while traveling down 12th Avenue South, why a couple of very out-of-place polar bears would be hanging out on the corner, frozen in mid-windup with a pawful of snowballs. And where are they getting those snowballs in this heat?! Rub your eyes if you must, but yes, right there at the end zone of a quaint little park in front of an apartment complex are these inexplicable concrete bears, who once stood in front of the Polar Bear Frozen Custard Shop in the 1930s, a "cool" spot across town in West End back in the day. There used to be four bears when they were the custard shop's mascots, but this corner only lets these two hang out in their suspended battle. However, a third bear of the set can be found just north of downtown at 1229 6th Ave North in the front yard of a private residence. Sadly, no evidence of a location for the fourth bear remains—we can only assume that he had had enough of the heat and moved back home to the much cooler climate of the North Pole.

The snowball-throwing bear has now become the mascot for the Edgehill neighborhood, where the boundary signs feature the figure.

SNOWBALL EFFECT

WHAT Snowball-throwing bears

WHERE 1125 Edgehill Ave & 1229 6th Ave. N. on Music Row

COST Free

PRO TIP One block away is Thai Esane, a popular lunch spot for Music Rowers.

Top: The bear on 6th Ave
Inset: Battling Edgehill bears

77 STIX

What's with the pickup sticks stuck in the ground in that roundabout?

Don't worry, many of us asked the same question when we sauntered past the Music City Center one day and saw a new art installation appropriately named *Stix* on the 8th Avenue roundabout. What could loosely be described as a handful of multicolored ginormous pickup sticks shoved end-first into the ground are actually twenty-seven red cedar wood poles jutting seventy feet into the air and laid out in an abstract and seemingly random pattern designed by artist Christian Moeller. Each pole is uniquely painted in different patterns of colored stripes of red, orange, blue, and green, and with a $750,000 price tag, that makes *Stix* the priciest piece of public art in Middle Tennessee.

The artwork is a tribute to the Native Americans who inhabited the land originally—the grass within the roundabout flora is a native grass, and the wood is the aforementioned red cedar. It's also with a ten-minute walking distance from other popular downtown sculptures, such as *Light Meander* at Riverfront Park (which is the chrome-themed giant snake shape of the Cumberland River by the amphitheater) and the *Ghost Ballet* (which is the red roller-coaster-looking one) across the river on the east bank near the football stadium.

Each pole is anchored fifteen feet into the Tennessee limestone below.

Stix roundabout

PICKUP STIX

WHAT *Stix* art

WHERE 8th Avenue and Korean Veterans Roundabout

COST Free

PRO TIP Nearby are Third Man Records and Jackalope Brewery.

SUICIDE ROCK

What is the Suicide Rock in the City Cemetery?

Make no bones about it, the City Cemetery is a creepy place. It's the longest continuously operated cemetery in Nashville and houses some famous folks, like Nashville founding father James Robertson and legendary songsmith Harlan Howard. As with any creepy cemetery, scary stories get started, and the fine line between truth and legend gets a tad blurry.

Such is the case with Ann Rawlins Sanders, a jilted lover who, according to local lore, committed suicide by jumping off a cliff after a fight with her husband, Charles Sanders. Sanders was so distraught that he reportedly arranged to have a chunk of the cliff that Ann jumped from to be placed on her grave, where it can still be seen today. In another chivalrous act, he also attached a lantern to the rock, as he knew that Ann was afraid of the dark.

But the story doesn't end there: back in the early 1900s, a cemetery keeper claimed that the true identity of the person buried under Ann Sanders's boulder was actually Edward Steele's wife, Lucy; Ann is instead supposedly buried in an adjacent plot. It has also been alleged that the boulder was simply selected by Edward (who was Secretary to the Board of Commissions in charge of building the State Capitol) from a nearby rock quarry that was being excavated for stone used in the Capitol's construction. As to what is true and what is fiction, that is lost to history and remains a secret that Nashville chooses to keep buried.

Nashville Founding Father James Robertson is entombed nearby in a family plot.

LUCY RAWLINS
STEELE
DIED MAY 4. 1847
ROCK PLACED OVER HER
GRAVE BY HER HUSBAND
EDWARD . STEELE

ROCK OF AGES

WHAT Suicide Rock

WHERE 1001 Fourth Ave. S.

COST Free

PRO TIP Head straight in from the 4th Ave entrance toward the visitor kiosk and the rock will be easily visible on the right.

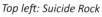

Top left: Suicide Rock
Top right: Headstone next to the rock

79 TABITHA TUDERS'S DISAPPEARANCE

What happened to Tabitha Tuders?

There are three notorious disappearance cases in recent Nashville history, the first of which was nine-year-old Marcia Trimble, who went missing in 1975 but whose case was solved in 2009 thanks to DNA evidence. The second was Holly Bobo, whose abduction from her own backyard in 2011 went national and appeared to be solved in 2014 when her remains were found and those responsible for her disappearance were arrested. The third one is Tabitha Tuders, a thirteen-year-old girl who disappeared on her way to her school bus stop, but her case remains unsolved.

On the morning of April 29, 2003, Tabitha left her house in East Nashville for a routine two-block walk to catch the bus, and somewhere on the way, she was taken. There was no commotion; no screams; and most vexing, no witnesses other than some vague claims that Tabitha was seen getting into a car, the colors of which have changed a number of times in the telling. There have also never been any remains recovered, leading some to speculate that Tabitha is perhaps still alive but preventing closure for her family if not. Hope is not lost, though—her family still has a banner of Tabitha flying on their front porch and believe that someday they will either have their daughter back or the answers to all the questions that have mounted in the meantime.

As of this printing, the reward is up to $51,000 for any information that leads to this case being closed.

East End neighborhood of East Nashville

WHERE'S TABITHA?

WHAT The disappearance of Tabitha Tuders

WHERE 1312 Lillian St.

COST N/A

PRO TIP Come forward if you know something!

The Investigation Discovery show *Disappeared* featured Tabitha's case in a 2018 episode.

Where did they film all those prison movies?

Nashville's pop culture scene could get a significant boost as a bustling filming location if state lawmakers ever decide to pass a tax incentive for the industry. Neighboring states, like Louisiana and Georgia, have become hotbeds for film and TV, and Nashville could also cash in on this opportunity. We've gotten a good start, though, with the ABC/CMT hit television drama *Nashville* having spent six years in production with all filming taking place on location. In addition, local resident Nicole Kidman has coerced a number of productions to take place in the area.

We also have a very recognizable face as the setting for a number of blockbuster movies, filmed at the former state prison in the west side of town. Designed by Enoch Guy Elliott and opened in 1898, this gothic monstrosity was in operation for 94 years until its controversial closure in 1992, after a federal judge dictated that no prisoner would ever be housed at that location again. At that point the prison became a popular filming location, appearing in *The Last Castle*, *Last Dance*, *Ernest Goes to Jail*, and *The Green Mile*, to name a few. Most scenes feature the gorgeous yet intimidating facade, as well as the courtyard in the interior (shown extensively in *The Last Castle*.)

Attempts at turning the prison into a museum periodically gain traction but have so far faltered

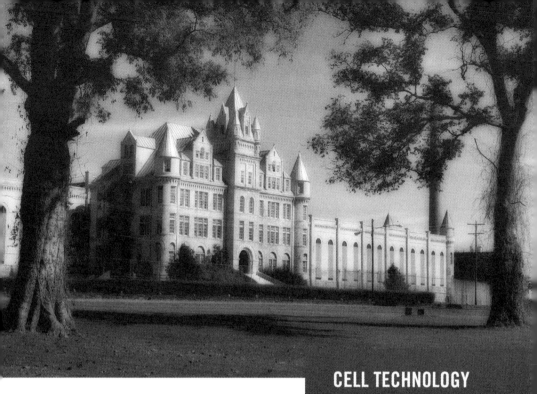

Tennessee State Prison. Photo credit Sean Smith.

CELL TECHNOLOGY

WHAT Tennessee state prison

WHERE 100 Bomar Blvd.

COST No admittance

PRO TIP An annual 5k sponsored by Tennessee DOC features a run through the prison courtyard.

The state prison is relatively easy to miss if you're driving down Briley—you'll need some eagle eyes to catch a quick glimpse—or you can take the risk and pull up the access road if you're feeling froggy. There is a guard station and an active prison behind it, so you will quickly be approached by authorities. But you may have just enough time for a good picture or two before they throw you into solitary confinement.

81 THIRD MAN RECORDING BOOTH

Where can someone cut a quick record to take home?

Tucked within an already fascinating display of vinyl records and music memorabilia at Third Man Records, Jack White's record label and store, is a unique feature that is one-of-a-kind in Nashville: a vinyl recording booth. No, this isn't like the ones seen at the mall where you sing along to your favorite song for a video camera, and they send a video to your email. Ladies and gentlemen, this 1947 Voice-o-Graph machine actually cuts your recording to a 6" vinyl phonograph record that you get to take home. The recordings are limited to around 150 seconds, so they're perfect for a short ditty, a personal message to a loved one, or random musings at a record store (the Third Man website claims to have had "marriage proposals, one-act plays, last will and testaments, Willie Nelson, jokes, and everything else in between in the booth," and encourages users to "be creative!") Recordings can also be converted to MP3 format to post on the Third Man Soundcloud, if so desired.

The booth operates on a first-come, first-served basis, costs $20 per song, and is one of those truly unique souvenirs that one is hard pressed to find in any other city in the world.

Third Man also offers myriad vinyl records, trinkets, and curiosities in the store.

ONE-OF-A-KIND SOUND EXPERIENCE

WHAT Third Man Recording Booth

WHERE 623 7th Ave. S.

COST Free to enter

PRO TIP Right around the corner is the studio of Dan Auerbach, lead singer of the band The Black Keys, located at 918 8th Ave. S.

Top left: Nashville's only vinyl recording booth
Top right: Controls of the booth

TREEHOUSE

Is the world's biggest treehouse in Nashville?

The world's biggest rumored treehouse IS indeed in Tennessee, but unfortunately it sits on private property 100 miles away from Nashville, in Crossville. However, there's a restaurant sitting right in the heart of East Nashville built around an actual family treehouse that might pique some curiosity. The appropriately named Treehouse restaurant is a casual little spot that sits on property that has been in co-owner Corey Ladd's family since the 1920s. Ladd, along with Matthew Spicher, opened the place in 2014 with a slight Central and South American theme to their tapas, as well as farm-to-table ingredients, a unique décor, and a constantly rolling classic rock soundtrack.

But back to the treehouse! Ladd's grandfather originally built the treehouse in the backyard of the residence on site, which became the centerpiece to the restaurant's hook. The attraction is right out on the back patio, painted with brightly colored murals and beckoning anyone who sees it looming amongst the branches to "Climb me!!" And as an added bonus, there's a bar integrated into the mix. There are a number of rooms in the treehouse where you can eat, including a second-story option for a larger gathering, but the highest chamber (the original treehouse) is off limits, unfortunately, because it's not quite up to code like the rest of the more current structure.

Across the street is the world famous Woodmont Studios and the trendy Five Points area, featured in the film *Ernest Scared Stupid*.

The Treehouse

FOR YOUR INNER CHILD

WHAT The Treehouse Nashville

WHERE 1011 Clearview Ave

COST Menu prices

PRO TIP Make dinner reservations well in advance.

83 TRUCK STOP KILLER

Where can a guy catch a serial killer around these parts?

With at least 25 truckers incarcerated for serial killings as of 2012, trucker killers are not as terribly uncommon as we might hope. The constant mobility and access to anonymous victims make for ideal opportunities if you're into that sort of thing. In Nashville, you can get your fill of this macabre attraction at the spot where, in June 2007, the Truck Stop Killer was arrested in his cab after dumping the body of Sara Hulbert at the same spot three weeks prior. In a stroke of truly random luck, Detective Pat Postiglione was working the case and just happened to be at the TA truck stop, gathering more evidence, when he spotted a truck similar to the one highlighted in the security cameras from the night of the murder. The detective sauntered on up to the cab, gave it a knock, and came face to face with Bruce Mendenhall, a career driver with a few sordid secrets. A search of the cab revealed women's clothes and other blood-stained items, and a DNA test linked Mendenhall to a number of other murders across the region, spanning all the way back to 1992. While Mendenhall isn't Nashville's most notorious murderer (this title most likely belongs to Paul Dennis Reid), this location and the proximity to downtown is a reminder of how close to home these tragedies can be. It also sparked some "We Are Nashville" pride that one of Nashville's finest caught a dangerous killer in our own backyard. Good eye, Detective Postiglione!

SERIAL CASE

WHAT Where they caught the killer

WHERE 111 N. 1st St.

COST Free to enter

PRO TIP Directions are squirrely—trust your GPS.

Top: The truckline where Mendenhall's truck was spotted
Inset: TA Travel Center downtown

Victims and evidence were also found at truck stops in Lebanon, TN, Birmingham, AL, and Indianapolis, IN.

Were the tunnels below Nashville once used for the Underground Railroad?

Hang around Nashville long enough and you'll hear whispers of one of the most persistent rumors: a vast network of underground tunnels that maze their way below downtown. One legend points to hidden passages used to transport bootleg hooch during Prohibition. Another tells of escape routes for politicians between the Capitol building and the Cumberland. More whispers talk of Nashville being part of the Underground Railroad and that mysterious sealed openings can be seen in basements of buildings still around today. Now, there is no denying that there are actual functioning tunnels running underneath all parts of Nashville, such as the usual sewage and drainage tunnels, as well as access tunnels for buildings like the Bridgestone Arena and the Music City Center. There are also miles of legitimate tunnels underneath the campuses of Vanderbilt and Tennessee State University, carrying steam and chilled water to the buildings.

No, the ones that are the subject of gossip are the covert pathways that have far less municipal record-keeping involved: hand chiseled human-trafficking tunnels and cadaver transport tubes that have no official documentation. So where are they if they exist at all?

That question has no definitive answer and is a prime Nashville secret. Skeptics say that any tunnels big enough to bootleg through or be a station in the Underground Railroad

---

There are also numerous riverbank contenders, such as the Wilson Spring storm tunnel feeding the Cumberland River via downtown and beyond.

Left: Tunnel ridge in Centennial Park
Right: Wilson Spring storm tunnel below
Ascend Amphitheater

would require explosives that would've easily drawn attention. Such tunneling would also have involved a very expensive and drawn-out process due to the limestone bedrock that the city sits on. As far as the Railroad goes, it has simply not been proved to have crossed through Nashville at all, so that hinders that hypothesis. And why bootleg through tunnels when you can just sneak around at night? When all is said and done, any extra tunnels used for clandestine purposes seem highly unlikely unless used for a private connection between neighboring buildings.

If you're wanting to experience how massive the known tunnel system is, visit the ridge near West Avenue and 25th Avenue North in Centennial Park, where the tunnel system shape, as well as a few revealing bricks, can be seen outlined in the grass.

85 UGLIEST STATUE IN EXISTENCE*

What in the world is that statue on I-65?!

Although only speculation, Nashville may indeed have the ugliest statue in the world on display on Interstate 65. Just south of downtown and Harding Place on the east side of the road, you will come across a man riding high on his horse, surrounded by a troop of 13 Confederate battle flags, and the most horrifically crazed smile cutting across his face as he wields his pistol at the passing traffic. This, ladies and gentlemen, is a grotesque tribute to Nathan Bedford Forrest, Confederate general and local historical figure most notably infamous for founding the KKK. Now, in fairness to Mr. Forrest, he attempted to disband the Klan when his initial intentions for the group went drastically awry. But no excuse can be made for what the organization became, and Mr. Forrest gets all the infamy. This 25-foot, gold-and-silver-leafed statue is the most reviled sculpture in Middle Tennessee, having been sprayed with graffiti, vandalized, and protested against countless times since its installation in 1998. However, owner and lawyer Bill Dorris maintains his right to display the statue on his own private property. It is protected by a gate and padlock, but you can get more than an eyeful from the interstate.

*According to the *Washington Post*.

Just south of the statue are the woods where Jim Reeves was killed in a plane crash inbound to Nashville in 1964.

The striking statue of Nathan Bedford Forrest. Photo credit Brent Moore.

UGLY IS AN UNDERSTATEMENT

WHAT The Nathan Bedford Forrest statue

WHERE 701D Hogan Rd., or on I-65 northbound near mile marker 77

COST Free

PRO TIP Trespassing is highly inadvisable.

86 UNITED RECORD PRESSING

I'm a super star—how fast can I get a record made?

If you're Jack White and the presses are being held for you, you can get a record done in a single day, just like he did on April 19, 2014, when he performed a song live on stage at his label, recorded it direct to acetate, ran it over to United Record Pressing (URP), and got the 45 vinyl single delivered back to his store for sale a mere hours later. Now, this is Jack White we're talking about, and that is a world record that he achieved, so things might be a little different for us laypeople.

The good news is, you'd be dealing with URP, the most experienced vinyl facility in the world, and it's located right in Nashville. In biz since 1949, URP has provided the vast majority of the vinyl albums on your shelf, most notably the Beatles first 7" singles, Dylan's *Highway 61 Revisited*, and Miles Davis's *Kind of Blue*. The original location on Chestnut Street also features one of Nashville's hidden jewels, The Motown Suite, where, during segregation, black artists would stay when in town on tour. This suite has been a temporary apartment for Marvin Gaye, Stevie Wonder, the Four Tops, the Supremes, and Smokey Robinson, to name a few. It still features the original furniture and a mysterious pair of shoes frozen in time since the '70s, as well. Legends like Hank Williams Jr. and Wayne Newton have also signed record deals in the "party room" of the building.

Alas, all good things come to an end as progress rears its ugly head—and so the story is the same for URP. With the resurgence of vinyl, the company had to upgrade to a far larger, less intriguing location that doesn't quite have the historical legacy or fascinating appeal that the original location has.

FOR THE RECORD

WHAT United Record Pressing

WHERE 453 Chestnut St. (original)

COST N/A

PRO TIP Call the plant and urge them to reopen tours.

Left: Record pressing at work
Right: Original site of United Record Pressing

As of this printing, there are no tours given at either location but have patience: plans are in the works for reopening the original location to the public.

87 WHERE THE LOCALS GO

All right, I know where the tourists go—but where do the locals go?

In any typical Nashville guide are a number of restaurants and hangouts that are always listed either due to legacy or popularity amongst the television shows, like the Loveless Café, Pancake Pantry, and the Bluebird Café. Not that these aren't great places to go, but they just aren't always frequented by the locals.

So where do the locals hang? Well first, we tend to stay away from downtown unless we have visitors in town. Depending on your vibe and resources, some of the more chill spots away from the bachelorette pedal taverns include Germantown, just north of downtown, with destinations like the Germantown Café, 5th and Taylor, and Bearded Iris Brewery. Across the river is Five Points, hub of the hipster scene, Margot, I Dream of Weenie (TV alert!), and the ever-ironic 3 Crow Bar. Nearby are The 5 Spot, a destined-to-be legendary music venue, and Red Door Saloon for some low-key action. Just down the road is arguably the best burger joint Nashville, The Pharmacy, hosting unique burgers and a kickin' outdoor biergarten. And next door to the Pharmacy is the Holland House, with unique cocktails to start/end your evening, as well as Mas Tacos, a hugely popular taco joint.

Now for a well-known secret: songwriters and major artists don't go downtown much either, instead hanging around Music Row to keep things on the downlow, at bars like the original flagship Tin Roof on Demonbreun Hill or down on Division at Winners or Losers, two adjacent bars catering to whatever level of esteem you're feeling that day. One block over is the Broadway Brewhouse, always a

LOCALS ONLY NO MORE

WHAT Where the Nashvillians hang

WHERE Nashville

COST Menu prices

PRO TIP Don't spend your entire trip on Broadway!

Top left: Winner's and Loser's on Division
Top right: 3 Crow Bar
Above left: Red Bicycle
Above right: M.L. Rose

winner in itself, while a short Uber ride away in "The Gulch" area of town are Whiskey Kitchen, one of Nashville's most distinctive menus, and Fin & Pearl, a seafood bistro.

Don't miss M.L. Rose, with multiple locations but the Melrose district housing the original. Across the street is The Sutler, a live music institution and multi-floor experience. And as you've already read, Santa's Pub is the bomb.

This is by no means a definitive list (and local opinions will vary!) but more so a quick guide if the downtown neon starts to dim and you want to discover Nashville's more honest element.

Far better food, music, and experiences are found off the beaten path from the tourist franchises of downtown.

WILLIE NELSON, FORTUNE TELLER

Willie, what does my future hold?

Sometimes when one is touring downtown Nashville, the neon and the honky tonkin' might cause one to begin to question many conundrums: past life decisions . . . current purpose in the world . . . bright or questionable futures. When this feeling overwhelms, there is only one man with the wisdom and the foresight to help regain one's personal balance in the world: Willie Nelson. Luckily, a coin-operated, mechanical Willie can be found in fine fortune-telling form confined to a booth at Music City Showcase on Broadway, most likely to keep any ganja smoke from leaking into the store. For a mere pittance, he'll take a deep drag and dispense psychedelic wisdom in a souvenir-sized slip of rolling paper suitable for small framing. Said tourist will return home with a worldly story sure to amaze friends and family.

The store is a solid option for all your gifting needs too, with Nashville-themed shot glasses, t-shirts, mugs, hats, toys, magnets, and thousands of other souvenirs from your journey. Toke your own tale at Music City Showcase with Willie and see what future he sees for you. Perhaps the first draft lyrics to his classic "Always on My Mind" will begin to make more sense: "I can always read your miiiiiiind . . . I can always read your mind."

ON THE ROAD AGAIN

WHAT Willie Nelson, the Fortune Teller

WHERE 323 Broadway

COST $1.00.

PRO TIP Make this a quick stop on your all-night Honky Tonkin' tour.

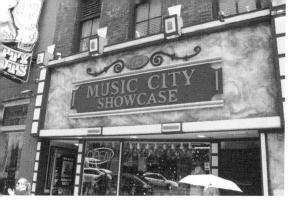

Left: Music City Showcase
Right: Willie's ready to tell a fortune or two

Willie the Fortune Teller was originally next door, at Dixieland, but has been replaced there by a mysterious outhouse with a particular guest wanting to serenade you.

89 WORST TRAIN WRECK IN U.S. HISTORY

Why is there a pile of train pieces on that one greenway trail?

Remember this classic math problem: If a train leaves Nashville at 7:07 p.m. on July 9, 1918, going 50 mph heading west toward Memphis while another train leaves Memphis and passes Bellevue at 7:09 p.m. going 60 mph, what time will they meet? The answer is 7:20 p.m., and the collision will result in the deadliest train wreck in American history, with 101 souls lost.

Both trains were behind schedule and trying to make up for lost time, but the blame lies mostly with a number of errors by the Memphis-bound train; it failed to wait near Centennial Park at the double-rail for the other train to pass. Instead, the trains collided at a bend in the tracks called Dutchman's Curve, where they couldn't see each other until much too late. The explosion was heard for miles around. Fires broke out in the surrounding cornfields while the screams of the dying overtook the silent countryside, and twisted onlookers by the tens of thousands came to see the bloodbath.

The *Nashville Tennessean* from June 10, 1918, reported that, "The cornfield on both sides of the track was trampled by many feet and littered with fragments of iron and wood hurled from the demolished cars. The dead lay here and there, grotesquely sprawling where they fell. The dying moaned

A DARK DAY IN NASHVILLE

WHAT The Dutchman's Curve Trainwreck

WHERE 22 White Bridge Road— Richland Creek Greenway

COST Free

PRO TIP On your walk, note the concrete pillars in the river that used hold the old tracks.

Top left: Stone supports of the original tracks
Top right: Remnants of the wreck
Above: The site of the crash

appeals for aid or, speechless, rolled their heads from side to side and writhed in agony. Everywhere there was blood and suffering and chaos."

Ninety of the 101 victims were African Americans on their way to work at a nearby munitions plant, but this news seems to have been overshadowed by the daily reports of lives lost in the horrific world war happening overseas.

Today, there is a memorial and very small park about a half-mile down the Richland Creek Greenway marking the spot of the crash with some train remnants that unfortunately cannot be confirmed to be from the wreck itself.

The street you're on is named for the "white bridge" at the entrance to the greenway.

90

WSM ANTENNA

Where are there diamonds in the sky?

One of the reasons that the Grand Ole Opry is a household name today was the nationwide reach of the program in the early days of radio, all thanks to a 50,000-watt transmission piping through this behemoth 878-foot radio antenna. In 1939, at the time when it was built, by the Blaw-Knox Company, it was the tallest antenna tower in the country (second only to the Eiffel Tower worldwide) and could broadcast WSM programs coast to coast. In fact, the groundbreaking tower was actually deemed too tall and had to be shortened to keep the radio waves from skipping off the atmosphere and thereby maximize its reach.

Off Concord Road south of downtown, the unmistakable diamond shape of the tower can be seen from pretty much any high point in the city, making for a somewhat deceiving distance gauge—it always looks closer than it really is until you get nearby and get a full feel for its gigantic presence. Most travelers through the area aren't aware of the power and history of this particular eye-catching structure, but if you stop in across the street at the Brentwood Library, you'll find an interactive marker out front that gives a thorough explanation of the details and design.

A quarter of a mile east down Concord Road is a convenience store that was featured in the Burt Reynolds movie *W.W. and the Dixie Dancekings.*

ANTENNESSEE

WHAT The WSM antenna

WHERE I-65 and Concord Rd.

COST N/A

PRO TIP Park across Concord for the best look at the antenna.

Top: WSM facilities
Inset: The diamond tower

91

ZERO MILESTONE

Where do all roads lead in Nashville?

Hidden amidst all of the features of Bicentennial Park is an easy-to-miss-unless-you-know-it's-there secret of the park and even the city as a whole. Look on the ground just south of the granite map at the edge of the grass and you'll see a stumpy metal post sticking out of an engraved stone that most folks probably just trip over and curse under their breath as they're walking toward the map. As the plaque will quickly tell you, the metal stump is more than just a tripwire. Since 1924, all mile markers of all Tennessee state highways have been measured from this very spot.

Zero milestones are common in many cities and states—you probably have one hidden in or around a major metropolitan area in your region. This one is simply Tennessee's version. Most milestones are based on the idea of the national marker just south of the White House in Washington, D.C., which was intended to be the point from which ALL roadways in the United States would be measured (although in the end, only D.C. roads are measured from there). The D.C. marker is itself an idealized version of the Golden Milestone in the ancient Roman Forum.

The marker is the zero point for the state highways, not interstates.

Zero Milestone marker

THE BEGINNING OF THE BEGINNING

WHAT The Zero Milestone marker

WHERE 600 James Robertson Pkwy, south side of park at bus drop-off area

COST Free

PRO TIP Browse around the giant granite map of Tennessee directly in front of the milestone.

SOURCES

1. https://www.atlasobscura.com/places/timothy-demonbreun-s-cave
2. http://www.bongojava.com/bongo-java/nun-bun/
3. https://www.tennessean.com/story/money/2016/12/02/11-years-later-nun-bun-mystery-remains/94743112/
4. https://www.wsmonline.com/history/
5. http://criminalminds.wikia.com/wiki/Bruce_Mendenhall
6. http://nashvilleguru.com/52988/patterson-house-nashville
7. https://www.tennessean.com/story/news/2016/11/06/exclusive-saber-tooth-bones-named-preds-get-new-home-bridgestone-arena/92829882/
8. http://nashvillepublicradio.org/post/curious-nashville-remembering-america-s-deadliest-train-crash#stream/0
9. http://sharetngov.tnsosfiles.com/tsla/exhibits/disasters/trains.htm
10. http://www.pbase.com/deadelvis/guitar
11. http://archive.gibson.com/GuitarTownWebsite/The%20GuitarTown%20Project/
12. http://nashvillepublicradio.org/post/curious-nashville-tunnels-live-legends-and-some-dont#stream/0
13. http://www.nashvillelifestyles.com/bestof/eight-things-you-need-to-know-about-nashvilles-stix-sculpture
14. https://www.nashvillescene.com/news/article/13044643/its-always-christmas-at-santas-pub-where-everybodys-naughty-but-nice
15. https://www.nashvillescene.com/news/article/13016007/tabitha-tuders
16. http://tnrenfest.com/directions.htm
17. http://americashauntedroadtrip.com/dyer-cemetery/
18. https://www.bizjournals.com/nashville/blog/real-estate/2014/07/what-you-dont-know-about-nashvilles-iconic-batman.html
19. https://www.tennessean.com/story/news/2014/10/21/super-skyline-batman-building-celebrates-years/17698193/
20. https://www.tennessean.com/story/news/2016/03/26/man-behind-batman-building-optimistic-new-nashville/82184472/
21. https://www.roadsideamerica.com/tip/24272
22. https://musicrow.com/2014/09/man-convicted-in-1989-music-row-murder-dies/
23. https://www.nashvillescene.com/news/article/13007520/with-a-bullet
24. http://www.rockandrollgps.com/jimi-hendrix-in-nashville/
25. https://www.tennessean.com/story/money/2016/08/08/efforts-begin-preserve-historic-jefferson-street-music-venue/87969542/
26. https://www.nashvillescene.com/news/pith-in-the-wind/article/13056408/if-the-geist-house-is-refurbished-could-we-finally-find-timothy-demonbreun
27. https://tdhouse.com/house-history/
28. http://www.wkrn.com/special-reports/haunted-tennessee/hank-williams-sr-known-to-haunt-ryman-auditorium-alley-behind-it/1057629802
29. https://www.nashvillescene.com/music/features/article/20863872/is-the-rymans-confederate-gallery-still-the-confederate-gallery
30. https://www.nashvillescene.com/news/pith-in-the-wind/article/20976369/rymans-confederate-sign-moved-to-museum-exhibit
31. http://www.prairieghosts.com/ryman.html
32. https://seeksghosts.blogspot.com/2013/10/haunted-ryman-auditorium.html
33. https://www.history.com/this-day-in-history/kkk-founded
34. http://skullsrainbowroom.com/history/

35. https://www.nashvillescene.com/news/article/13063881/with-the-reopening-of-skulls-rainbow-room-in-printers-alley-we-visit-a-story-of-music-burlesque-historic-preservation-and-murder
36. https://tnstateparks.com/parks/about/bicentennial-mall
37. https://rootsrated.com/stories/a-guide-to-kayaking-and-island-camping-on-percy-priest-lake
38. http://www.percypriestlake.org/percy-priest-lake/
39. https://suburbanturmoil.com/tennessee-state-museum/2016/09/13/
40. http://www.nashvillelifestyles.com/entertainment/nashville-zoo-renovations
41. https://www.nashvillesymphony.org/about/schermerhorn-symphony-center/building-art/
42. https://rkpowers.wordpress.com/2012/01/23/looking-back-etc-part-4/
43. https://www.ryman.com/history/opry/
44. http://www.scarrittbennett.org/education/soulwork/labyrinth/
45. http://www.nashville.gov/Arts-Commission/Experience-Art/Metro-Public-Art-Collection/Bike-Racks.aspx
46. http://www.pbase.com/charliedoggett/catfishart&page=all
47. https://www.urpressing.com/history/
48. http://www.tnledger.com/editorial/Article.aspx?id=84576
49. https://www.tennessean.com/story/sports/nhl/predators/2018/04/12/nash-ville-predators-why-do-fans-throw-catfish-nhl-stanley-cup-playoffs-bridgestone-arena/508025002/
50. http://nashvillepublicradio.org/post/curious-nashville-glimpses-forgotten-zoo-suburban-green-hills#stream/0
51. https://cootersplace.com/cooters-nashville/
52. https://www.geocaching.com/geocache/GC206AR_shelby-park-cave-spring?guid=44900d5f-b5f9-409b-8087-44236c69a08b
53. https://www.tennessean.com/story/news/2018/01/11/oprah-president-win-frey-barbershop-nashville/1015204001/
54. https://dpchurch.com/church/history/
55. https://www.nashvilledowntown.com/go/downtown-presbyterian-church
56. https://www.camelsandchocolate.com/nashville-murals/
57. https://thirdmanrecords.com/news/record-store-day-at-third-man-records/
58. https://www.tennessean.com/story/life/shopping/ms-cheap/2015/11/27/renovation-rejuvenates-childrens-library/76302730/
59. http://www.davisbaby.com/tag/library/
60. https://www.musicianshalloffame.com/
61. https://suburbanturmoil.com/bison-meadow-one-of-nashvilles-best-kept-secrets-2/2015/05/04/
62. https://www.flickr.com/photos/brent_nashville/37445658951
63. https://www.nashvilledowntown.com/go/tennessee-state-capitol
64. https://www.wilsonpost.com/community/quarry-attracts-divers-from-across-mid-south/article_b44dab06-07bd-5067-92ca-d28cdfa1dea0.html
65. https://www.nashvillepost.com/business/development/article/20441905/atkins-statue-unveiled-downtown
66. http://www.scottymoore.net/studio_mcgavock.html
67. https://www.nashville.gov/Portals/0/SiteContent/MHZC/docs/Design%20guide-lines%20and%20HB/Landmark%202017.pdf
68. http://darkdestinations.blogspot.com/2009/03/curse-of-grand-ole-opry.html
69. http://people.com/country/brett-eldredge-pee-plaque-warner-music-nashville/
70. https://steemit.com/art/@katecloud/the-mural-i-created-over-a-wall-of-open-silverstein-books

71. https://www.tennessean.com/story/news/local/davidson%20/2016/04/26/nashvilles-centennial-park-train-could-restored-run-again/83400574/
72. https://www.tennessean.com/story/news/local/2016/08/19/nashvilles-centennial-park-train-okd-restoration-operation/88966110/
73. http://www.wsmv.com/story/25496273/man-leads-effort-to-build-full-scale-replica-of-millenium-falcon
74. https://www.tennessean.com/story/money/industries/music/2017/10/21/rca-studio-a-iconic-signs-after-nearly-50-years/787238001/
75. http://nashvilleguru.com/13815/the-treehouse-nashville
76. http://nashvillepublicradio.org/post/curious-nashville-how-engineering-failure-led-riverfront-park#stream/0
77. https://www.nashvillescene.com/arts-culture/article/13002259/voices-carry
78. https://www.tennessean.com/story/entertainment/music/2015/02/05/nashville-then-burt-reynolds-movie/22868579/
79. Manley, Roger. WEIRD TENNESSEE: Your Travel Guide to Tennessee's Local Legends and Best Kept Secrets. Sterling, 2011
80. Douglas, Mason. NOW YOU KNOW NASHVILLE. Wild Cataclysm, 2013
81. http://www.thenashvillecitycemetery.org/180060_steel.htm

INDEX